Real English *for*
HOTEL STAFF

기본편 Michael A. Putlack, 김진숙 저

DARAKWON

개정판

Real English *for*
HOTEL STAFF 기본편

지은이 Michael A. Putlack, 김진숙
펴낸이 정규도
펴낸곳 (주)다락원

초판 1쇄 발행 2016년 2월 15일
2판 1쇄 발행 2026년 1월 26일

편집 김태연, 조상익
감수 노선희(백석대 관광학부 교수)
디자인 김민지, 김예지

다락원 경기도 파주시 문발로 211
내용문의 (02) 736-2031 내선 550
구입문의 (02) 736-2031 내선 250~252
Fax (02) 732-2037
출판등록 1977년 9월 16일 제406-2008-000007호

ISBN 978-89-277-8122-6 14740
　　　978-89-277-8121-9 14740 (set)

http://www.darakwon.co.kr
다락원 홈페이지를 방문하시면 상세한 출판 정보와 함께 MP3 자료 등의 다양한 어학 정보를 얻으실 수 있습니다.

To the Students

최근 호텔업계에서는 입사 경쟁이 매우 치열합니다. 따라서 호텔에 취직하고자 하는 이들은 최대한 높은 경쟁력을 갖추어야 합니다. 호텔업계에서 필수적인 경쟁력 중 하나는 영어 말하기 능력입니다. 영어는 세계 공용어이며, 호텔에 숙박하는 고객 중 다수가 영어로 의사소통을 하려고 합니다. 따라서 대부분의 호텔들이 영어를 잘하는 지원자, 그중에서도 특히 영어로 고객과 의사소통을 원활하게 할 수 있는 지원자를 채용할 가능성이 높습니다.

Real English for Hotel Staff 기본편은 호텔 취업에 필수적인 영어 표현을 학습할 수 있도록 구성되어 있습니다. 본 교재의 유닛들은 호텔에서 일어날 수 있는 다양한 상황을 그 배경으로 삼고 있습니다. 예약 접수, 체크인, 체크아웃, 룸서비스 주문, 그리고 기타 서비스와 관련된 다양한 주제들을 다루고 있습니다. 또한 호텔리어에게 꼭 필요한 핵심 단어 및 표현들도 제공하고 있습니다.

Real English for Hotel Staff 기본편은 일차적으로 대학 수업용 교재로 개발되었지만, 독학도 가능하도록 구성되어 있습니다. 본 교재는 말하기와 듣기에 중점을 두고 있으며, 독해 및 기초 문법을 다루는 코너도 수록하고 있습니다. **Real English for Hotel Staff 기본편**으로 꾸준히 학습한다면, 자신도 모르는 사이에, 상황에 따른 다양한 영어 표현을 구사할 수 있게 될 것입니다.

Real English for Hotel Staff 기본편을 통해 영어 실력도 쌓고 호텔 취업의 꿈도 이루시기를 진심으로 기원합니다.

저자 일동

Contents

각 유닛은 주제와 관련된 워밍업 활동으로 시작되며, 두 개의 대화문을 중심으로 중요한 단어, 표현, 문법 사항을 학습할 수 있도록 구성되어 있습니다. 뿐만 아니라 말하기와 듣기 학습을 할 수 있는 활동도 마련되어 있습니다. 마지막으로, 해당 주제와 관련된 독해 지문을 읽어봄으로써 유닛을 마무리할 수 있습니다.

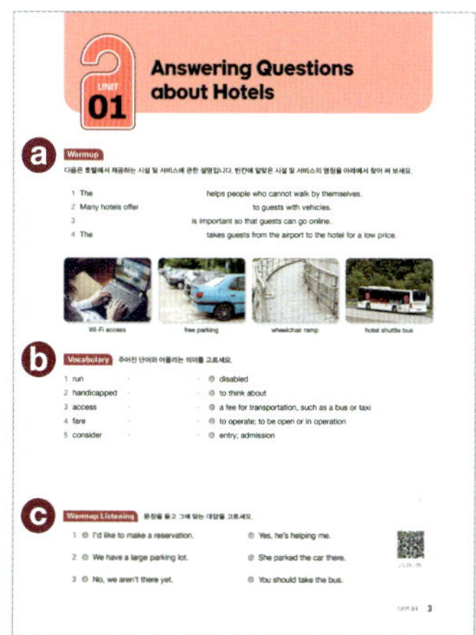

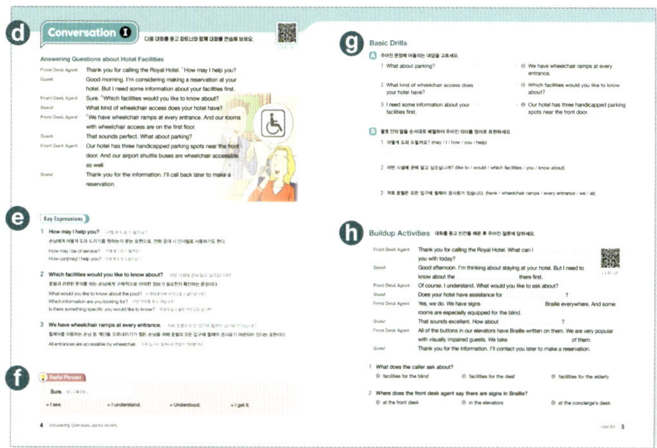

ⓐ Warmup
주제와 관련된 쉽고 흥미로운 활동을 통해 학습을 준비합니다.

ⓑ Vocabulary
대화문의 핵심 단어를 미리 학습해 봅니다.

ⓒ Warmup Listening
대화문의 기본 표현을 미리 학습해 봅니다.

ⓓ Conversation I, II
대화문을 파트너와 함께 연습해 봅니다.

ⓔ Key Expressions
대화문의 핵심 표현 세 가지를 집중적으로 학습합니다.

ⓕ Useful Phrases
대화문과 관련된 추가적인 표현을 학습합니다.

ⓖ Basic Drills
간단한 활동을 통해 배운 내용을 확인합니다.

ⓗ Buildup Activities
받아쓰기 및 문제 풀기를 통해 앞서 배운 내용을 확실하게 이해합니다.

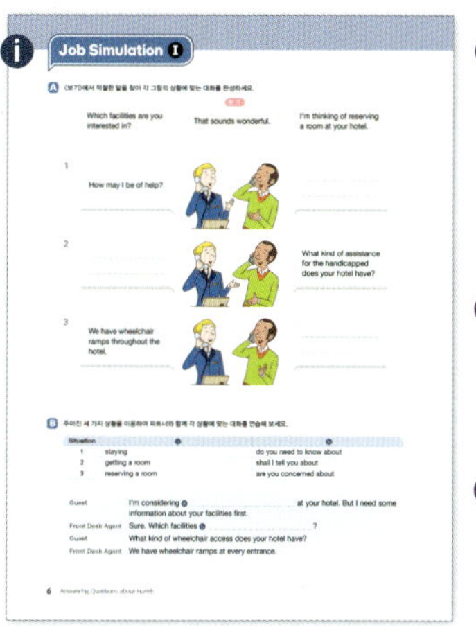

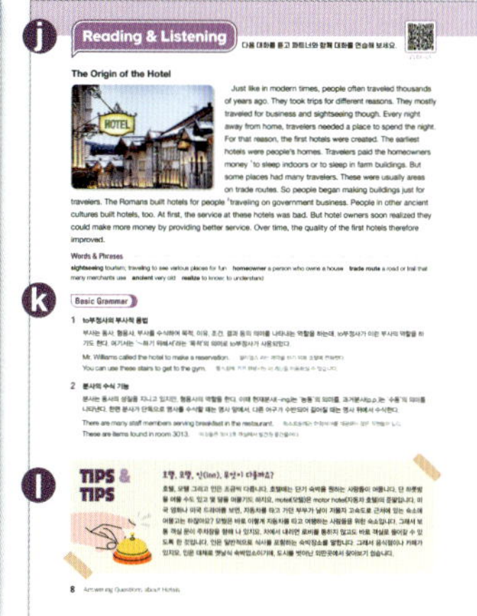

ⓘ Job Simulation I, II
핵심 표현을 응용하여 배운 내용을 상황에 맞게 적용시켜 봅니다.

ⓙ Reading & Listening
읽기 및 듣기를 통해 주제와 관련된 배경지식을 쌓습니다.

ⓚ Basic Grammar
지문의 기본 문법 사항을 학습합니다.

ⓛ TIPS & TIPS
한글로 제공되는 흥미로운 토막글을 통해 해당 분야에 관한 상식을 넓힐 수 있습니다.

Plan of the Book

Unit	Topic	Situations	Language Focus
01	Answering Questions about Hotels	❶ Answering Questions about Hotel Facilities ❷ Describing How to Get to the Hotel from the Airport	- greeting callers and asking how to help them - describing hotel facilities in detail - giving hours of operation - giving options with "either A or B" - telling how long it will take to get somewhere
02	Reservations	❶ Taking Reservations ❷ Changing Reservations	- describing special offers - making telephone reservations - asking how to spell names - asking people to repeat information - changing dates on reservations
03	Check-in Service	❶ Check-in Service for Reservations Made on a Website ❷ Check-in Service for Walk-ins	- welcoming guests at check-in - using "would you prefer" to learn preferences - expressing regret to inconvenienced guests - handling walk-in guests - requesting identification
04	Giving Essential Information about Hotel Services	❶ Providing Essential Information about Rooms and Services ❷ Explaining Hotel Facilities and Services	- describing the locations of hotel facilities - answering questions about facilities - naming hotel facilities and their floors
05	Giving Local Information	❶ Giving Advice about Local Travel ❷ Advising Guests on Visitor Attractions	- talking about public transportation - using "need to" for requirements - making recommendations of places to see - making suggestions with "why don't you" - using "let me" to describe actions
06	Restaurant & Bar Service	❶ Breakfast at the Restaurant ❷ Drinks at the Bar	- greeting guests - using "would you like to" to ask questions - naming various types of foods - offering to serve guests - describing the contents of drinks
07	Hotel Facilities	❶ At the Fitness Center ❷ At the Business Center	- asking for room numbers - giving directions - asking "do you know how to"
08	Room Service	❶ Taking Room Service Orders on the Phone ❷ Making Special Deliveries	- taking telephone orders - asking questions with "how about" - giving total costs - asking for confirmation with "~, right?" - using "shall I"

09	Housekeeping Service	❶ Providing Housekeeping Services ❷ Handling Complaints about Room Problems	- asking polite questions - making apologies - asking for additional information - solving problems by describing future actions with "will"
10	Mistakes and Complaints	❶ Handling Complaints about Wrong Rooms ❷ Taking Care of Complaints at a Restaurant	- apologizing for mistakes - providing upgrades to guests - asking for more information regarding complaints - solving problems with "let me"
11	Helping Guests	❶ Lost and Found Service ❷ Emergencies and First Aid	- asking for descriptions of items - giving lost items back to guests - asking about injuries - calling ambulances - keeping guests calm
12	Checkout Service	❶ Checkout Service ❷ Handling Disputed Charges	- asking how guests enjoyed their stays - preparing bills for guests - helping guests leave hotels - asking about charges on bills - removing incorrect charges from bills

※ NCS(국가직무능력표준) 능력단위와의 연계성

분류	능력단위 및 분류번호	능력단위 요소	연계 Unit
직업기초능력 〉 **의사소통능력**	기초 외국어 능력 (A-2-마.)	외국어 듣기 일상생활의 회화 활용	UNIT 01-12
12. 이용·숙박·여행·오락 〉 03. 관광·레저 〉 02. 숙박서비스 〉 **02. 객실관리**	01. 객실 예약 접수 (1203020201_13v1)	객실 및 부대시설 이용정보 파악하기	UNIT 01
		예약 현황 확인하기 예약 변경하기	UNIT 02
	02. 체크 인(Check In) (1203020202_13v1)	고객 응대하기 등록카드 작성하기	UNIT 03
		객실 키 발급 및 정보 제공하기	UNIT 04
	03. 재실고객 관리 (1203020203_13v1)	고객 요청 사항 처리하기 고객 불평 접수하기	UNIT 10
	04. 체크 아웃(Check Out) (1203020206_13v1)	추가 사용 내역 확인하기 최종 내역 계산하기 환송하기	UNIT 12
	08. 하우스키핑 정비 (1203020208_13v1)	오더 테이킹(Order Taking) 처리하기	UNIT 09
	09. 하우스키핑 관리 (1203020209_13v1)	호텔 습득물 처리하기(Lost and Found)	UNIT 11
12. 이용·숙박·여행·오락 〉 03. 관광·레저 〉 02. 숙박서비스 〉 **05. 접객서비스**	03. 벨 데스크 (1203020503_13v1)	객실 안내하기	UNIT 04
	04. 컨시어지(concierge) (1203020504_13v1)	요청 정보 제공하기	UNIT 05
	08. 고객 서비스 센터 (1203020508_13v1)	호텔 상품 안내하기 객실 고객의 주문받기	UNIT 08
	09. 당직 (1203020509_13v1)	긴급 상황 업무 처리하기	UNIT 11

UNIT 01
Answering Questions about Hotels

다음은 호텔에서 제공하는 시설 및 서비스에 관한 설명입니다. 빈칸에 알맞은 시설 및 서비스의 명칭을 아래에서 찾아 써 보세요.

1 The ___________________ helps people who cannot walk by themselves.

2 Many hotels offer ___________________ to guests with vehicles.

3 ___________________ is important so that guests can go online.

4 The ___________________ takes guests from the airport to the hotel for a low price.

Wi-Fi access

free parking

wheelchair ramp

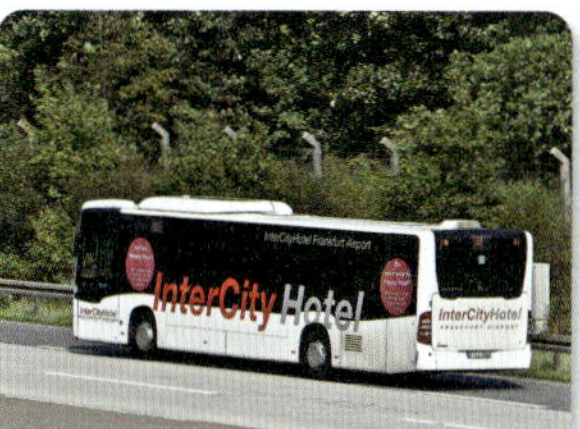

hotel shuttle bus

Vocabulary 주어진 단어와 어울리는 의미를 고르세요.

1 run •　　　• ⓐ disabled

2 handicapped •　　　• ⓑ to think about

3 access •　　　• ⓒ a fee for transportation, such as a bus or taxi

4 fare •　　　• ⓓ to operate; to be open or in operation

5 consider •　　　• ⓔ entry; admission

Warmup Listening 문장을 듣고 그에 맞는 대답을 고르세요.

1 ⓐ I'd like to make a reservation.　　　ⓑ Yes, he's helping me.

2 ⓐ We have a large parking lot.　　　ⓑ She parked the car there.

3 ⓐ No, we aren't there yet.　　　ⓑ You should take the bus.

🎧 01-01

Conversation I

다음 대화를 듣고 파트너와 함께 대화를 연습해 보세요.

🎧 01-02

Answering Questions about Hotel Facilities

Front Desk Agent	Thank you for calling the Royal Hotel. [1]How may I help you?
Guest	Good morning. I'm considering making a reservation at your hotel. But I need some information about your facilities first.
Front Desk Agent	Sure. [2]Which facilities would you like to know about?
Guest	What kind of wheelchair access does your hotel have?
Front Desk Agent	[3]There are wheelchair ramps at every entrance. And our rooms with wheelchair access are on the first floor.
Guest	That sounds perfect. What about parking?
Front Desk Agent	Our hotel has three handicapped parking spots near the front door. Our airport shuttle buses are wheelchair accessible as well.
Guest	Thank you for the information. I'll visit your website later to make a reservation.

1 How may I help you?   어떻게 도와 드릴까요?

손님에게 어떤 도움이 필요한지 묻는 표현으로, 전화 응대 시 인사말로 사용하기도 한다.

How may I be of service?   어떻게 도와 드릴까요?
How can [may] I help you?   어떻게 도와 드릴까요?

2 Which facilities would you like to know about?   어떤 시설에 관해 알고 싶으십니까?

호텔과 관련된 문의를 하는 손님에게 구체적으로 어떠한 정보가 필요한지 확인하는 문장이다.

What would you like to know about the pool?   수영장에 관해 무엇이 알고 싶으십니까?
Which information are you looking for?   어떤 정보를 찾고 계십니까?
Is there something specific you would like to know?   특별히 알고 싶은 것이 있으십니까?

3 There are wheelchair ramps at every entrance.   모든 입구에 휠체어 경사로가 있습니다.

휠체어를 이용하는 손님 등 계단을 오르내리기가 힘든 손님을 위해서 모든 입구에 휠체어 경사로가 마련되어 있다는 표현이다.

All entrances are accessible by wheelchair.   모든 입구는 휠체어로 진입이 가능합니다.

💡 Useful Phrases

Sure. 네. [그렇군요.]

= I see.   = Understood.   = I understand.   = I get it.

Basic Drills

A 주어진 문장에 어울리는 대답을 고르세요.

1 What about parking?

2 What kind of wheelchair access does your hotel have?

3 I need some information about your facilities first.

ⓐ There are wheelchair ramps at every entrance.

ⓑ Which facilities would you like to know about?

ⓒ Our hotel has three handicapped parking spots near the front door.

B 괄호 안의 말을 순서대로 배열하여 주어진 의미를 영어로 표현하세요.

1 어떻게 도와 드릴까요? (may / I / how / you / help)

➡

2 어떤 시설에 관해 알고 싶으십니까? (like to / would / which facilities / you / know about)

➡

3 모든 입구에 휠체어 경사로가 있습니다. (are / wheelchair ramps / every entrance / there / at)

➡

Buildup Activities 대화를 듣고 빈칸을 채운 후 주어진 질문에 답하세요.

Front Desk Agent	Thank you for calling the Royal Hotel. What can I _____ you with today?
Guest	Good afternoon. I'm thinking about staying at your hotel. But I need to know about the _____ there first.
Front Desk Agent	Of course. I understand. What would you like to ask about?
Guest	Does your hotel have assistance for _____?
Front Desk Agent	Yes, we do. There are signs _____ Braille everywhere. And some rooms are especially equipped for the blind.
Guest	That sounds excellent. How about _____?
Front Desk Agent	All of the buttons in our elevators have Braille written on them. We are very popular with visually impaired guests. We take _____ of them.
Guest	Thank you for the information. I'll contact you later to make a reservation.

🎧 01 - 03

1 What does the caller ask about?

ⓐ facilities for the blind

ⓑ facilities for the deaf

ⓒ facilities for the elderly

2 Where does the front desk agent say there are signs in Braille?

ⓐ at the front desk   **ⓑ** in the elevators   **ⓒ** at the concierge's desk

Conversation 

다음 대화를 듣고 파트너와 함께 대화를 연습해 보세요.

🎧 01 - 04

Describing How to Get to the Hotel from the Airport

Front Desk Agent	Royal Hotel. This is Cindy speaking. How may I be of service?
Guest	Hello. I will be going to your hotel from the airport. What's the best way to get there?
Front Desk Agent	[1]The easiest way is to take our shuttle bus. It leaves the airport every hour on the hour. It runs from 7:00 AM until 7:00 PM.
Guest	My plane is going to arrive at 8:30 PM, so I can't take the shuttle bus.
Front Desk Agent	[2]In that case, you can take either a city bus or a rideshare.
Guest	Can you tell me more about both of them?
Front Desk Agent	Of course. Ordering a car through a rideshare service will cost around $25. [3]It takes around thirty minutes to get here by car. As for the bus, it's a 50-minute trip on the number 7 bus.
Guest	I think I'll just order a car. I appreciate the assistance.

Key Expressions

1 The easiest way is to take our shuttle bus.   가장 편한 방법은 저희 셔틀 버스를 타시는 것입니다.

어떤 목적지에 가기 위한 최적의 교통 수단을 안내하는 표현으로, the best option(가장 좋은 선택), the fastest way(가장 빠른 방법) 등을 사용하여 나타낼 수도 있다. 또한 'by + 교통 수단'을 사용해 '~을 타고'라는 뜻을 나타낼 수도 있다.

Your best option is to use our shuttle bus.   가장 좋은 선택은 저희 셔틀 버스를 이용하시는 것입니다.
The fastest way to get there is by car.   그곳에 가는 가장 빠른 방법은 차를 타시는 것입니다.

2 In that case, you can take either a city bus or a rideshare.
그렇다면, 시내 버스나 승차 공유 서비스를 이용하실 수 있습니다.

손님에게 이용할 수 있는 교통 수단이 두 가지 있다고 설명할 때 사용하며, 보통 두 개의 선택 사항은 either A or B(A나 B)라는 표현으로 나타낸다.

In your situation, you can get there either by subway or bus.   손님의 경우에는 지하철이나 버스를 타고 그곳에 가실 수 있습니다.

3 It takes around thirty minutes to get here by car.   차를 타고 여기까지 오시는데 약 30분이 걸립니다.

특정 교통 수단을 이용하여 목적지까지 가는데 걸리는 시간을 안내하는 표현이다. '(시간이) 걸리다'라는 의미의 동사 take 뒤에 소요 시간을 넣는다. 참고로 '걸어서'라는 뜻을 나타낼 때는 on foot을 사용한다.

It will take an hour to get to the airport by train.   기차를 타고 공항까지 가는데는 한 시간이 걸릴 것입니다.
It takes 5 to 10 minutes on foot.   걸어서 5분에서 10분이 걸립니다.

💡 Useful Phrases

고맙습니다.

= I appreciate it.   = Thank you (very much).   = I am grateful for it.   = I can't thank you enough.

Basic Drills

A 주어진 문장에 어울리는 대답을 고르세요.

1 I can't take the shuttle bus. •

            • **ⓐ** The easiest way is to take our shuttle bus.

2 Can you tell me more about both of them? •

            • **ⓑ** Ordering a car through a rideshare service will cost around $25.

3 What's the best way to get there? •

            • **ⓒ** In that case, you can take either a city bus or a rideshare.

B 괄호 안의 말을 순서대로 배열하여 주어진 의미를 영어로 표현하세요.

1 가장 편한 방법은 저희 셔틀 버스를 타시는 것입니다. (to take / way / the easiest / is / our shuttle bus)

   → ____

2 그렇다면, 시내 버스나 승차 공유 서비스를 이용하실 수 있습니다.
(a city bus / you / either / in that case / can take / or / a rideshare)

   → ____

3 차를 타고 여기까지 오시는데 약 30분이 걸립니다. (to get here / thirty minutes / around / by car / it takes)

   → ____

Buildup Activities 대화를 듣고 빈칸을 채운 후 주어진 질문에 답하세요.

Front Desk Agent	Royal Hotel. You are speaking with Chris. How may I assist you?
Guest	Hello. I'm going to go from the ________________ to your hotel. What's the fastest way there?
Front Desk Agent	The ________________ is to take our shuttle bus. You can catch it in front of Exit 5. It operates from 6:00 AM until 8:00 PM.
Guest	My plane is arriving ________________, so I can't use the shuttle bus.
Front Desk Agent	Hmm . . . You'd better take a bus or a rideshare then.
Guest	Can you give me some ________________ about each one?
Front Desk Agent	Sure. It will ________________ about $30 to come here in a rideshare. It will take about 25 minutes if you ride in a car. If you take the bus, get on the number 10 bus. It will be a one-hour ride.
Guest	The rideshare sounds ________________ the bus. Thanks for telling me about everything.

🎧 01 - 06

1 What time does the shuttle bus stop running?
- **ⓐ** at 6:00 PM
- **ⓑ** at 8:00 PM
- **ⓒ** at 10:00 PM

2 How will the caller go to the hotel?
- **ⓐ** by bus
- **ⓑ** in a rideshare
- **ⓒ** by shuttle bus

Job Simulation **I**

A 〈보기〉에서 적절한 말을 찾아 각 그림의 상황에 맞는 대화를 완성하세요.

보기

Which facilities are you interested in?

That sounds wonderful.

I'm thinking of reserving a room at your hotel.

1

2

3

B 주어진 세 가지 상황을 이용하여 파트너와 함께 각 상황에 맞는 대화를 연습해 보세요.

Situation	ⓐ	ⓑ
1	staying	do you need to know about
2	getting a room	shall I tell you about
3	reserving a room	are you concerned about

Guest   I'm considering ⓐ __________ at your hotel. But I need some information about your facilities first.

Front Desk Agent   Sure. Which facilities ⓑ __________?

Guest   What kind of wheelchair access does your hotel have?

Front Desk Agent   We have wheelchair ramps at every entrance.

Job Simulation II

A 〈보기〉에서 적절한 말을 찾아 각 그림의 상황에 맞는 대화를 완성하세요.

보기

1

2

3

B 주어진 세 가지 상황을 이용하여 파트너와 함께 각 상황에 맞는 대화를 연습해 보세요.

Situation	ⓐ	ⓑ	ⓒ
1	How should I go there	5:00 AM until 8:00 PM	half an hour
2	What's the easiest way to go there	7:00 to 7:00	no more than 20 minutes
3	How can I get there the easiest	noon to 8:00 PM	approximately 15 minutes

Guest	Hello. I will be going to your hotel from the airport. ⓐ _______?
Front Desk Agent	The easiest way is to take our shuttle bus. It runs from ⓑ _______.
Guest	My plane is going to arrive at 8:30 PM, so I can't take the shuttle bus.
Front Desk Agent	In that case, you can take a rideshare. It takes ⓒ _______ to get here by car.

🎧 01-06

The Origin of the Hotel

Just like in modern times, people often traveled thousands of years ago. They took trips for different reasons. They mostly traveled for business and sightseeing though. Every night away from home, travelers needed a place to spend the night. For that reason, the first hotels were created. The earliest hotels were people's homes. Travelers paid homeowners money [1]to sleep indoors or to sleep in farm buildings. But some places had many travelers. These were usually areas on trade routes. So people began making buildings just for travelers. The Romans built hotels for people [2]traveling on government business. People in other ancient cultures built hotels, too. At first, the service at these hotels was bad. But hotel owners soon realized they could make more money by providing better service. Over time, the quality of the first hotels therefore improved.

Words & Phrases

sightseeing tourism; traveling to see various places for fun **homeowner** a person who owns a house **trade route** a road or trail that many merchants use **ancient** very old **realize** to know; to understand

Basic Grammar

1 to부정사의 부사적 용법

부사는 동사, 형용사, 부사를 수식하여 목적, 이유, 조건, 결과 등의 의미를 나타내는데, to부정사가 이런 부사의 역할을 하기도 한다. 여기서는 '~하기 위해서'라는 '목적'의 의미로 to부정사가 사용되었다.

Mr. Williams called the hotel to make a reservation.   윌리엄스 씨는 예약을 하기 위해 호텔에 전화했다.
You can use these stairs to get to the gym.   헬스장에 가기 위해서는 이 계단을 이용하실 수 있습니다.

2 분사의 수식 기능

분사는 동사의 성질을 지니고 있지만, 형용사의 역할을 한다. 이때 현재분사(-ing)는 '능동'의 의미를, 과거분사(p.p.)는 '수동'의 의미를 나타낸다. 한편 분사가 단독으로 명사를 수식할 때는 명사 앞에서, 또는 다른 어구가 수반되어 길어질 때는 명사 뒤에서 수식한다.

There are many staff members serving breakfast in the restaurant.   레스토랑에서 많은 직원들이 아침 식사를 서빙하고 있다.
These are items found in room 3013.   이것들은 3013호 객실에서 발견된 물건들이다.

TIPS & TIPS

호텔, 모텔, 인(inn). 무엇이 다를까요?

호텔, 모텔 그리고 인은 조금씩 다릅니다. 호텔에는 단기 숙박을 원하는 사람들이 머뭅니다. 단 하룻밤을 머물 수도 있고 몇 달을 머물기도 하지요. motel(모텔)은 motor hotel(자동차 호텔)의 준말입니다. 미국 영화나 미국 드라마를 보면, 자동차를 타고 가던 부부가 날이 저물자 고속도로 근처에 있는 숙소에 머물고는 하잖아요? 모텔은 바로 이렇게 자동차를 타고 여행하는 사람들을 위한 숙소입니다. 그래서 보통 객실 문이 주차장을 향해 나 있지요. 차에서 내리면 로비를 통하지 않고도 바로 객실로 들어갈 수 있도록 한 것입니다. 인은 일반적으로 식사 서비스가 포함된 숙박 장소를 말합니다. 그래서 음식점이나 카페가 있지요. 인은 대체로 옛날식 숙박업소이기에, 도시를 벗어난 외딴곳에서 찾아보기 쉽습니다.

Reservations

UNIT 02

Warmup

다음은 호텔을 예약하고자 하는 고객들의 이야기입니다. 각 고객이 예약할 객실을 사진에서 고르세요.

1 "My husband and I are traveling on our honeymoon."

2 "I'm traveling by myself and don't want to spend a lot of money."

3 "I'm traveling with my coworker on a business trip."

ⓐ single room

ⓑ double room

ⓒ twin room

Vocabulary 주어진 단어와 어울리는 의미를 고르세요.

1 repeat •   • ⓐ to need

2 complimentary •   • ⓑ to say or do again

3 discounted •   • ⓒ on sale; being sold at a lower price

4 require •   • ⓓ to make sure

5 guarantee •   • ⓔ free

Warmup Listening 문장을 듣고 그에 맞는 대답을 고르세요.

1 ⓐ Yes, you reserved a double room.   ⓑ Yes, we have three empty rooms now.

2 ⓐ That's S-M-I-T-H.   ⓑ It's Mark Powell.

3 ⓐ I need to stay two days longer.   ⓑ That's right. I changed it.

🎧 02-01

다음 대화를 듣고 파트너와 함께 대화를 연습해 보세요.

🎧 02-02

Taking Reservations

Guest Hello. Your website is down, and I'd like to make a reservation for this weekend. Do you have any rooms available?

Reservation Clerk Let me check . . . Yes, several rooms are still available. We also have a special promotional offer this weekend.

Guest Really? Could you tell me about it?

Reservation Clerk Sure. [1] You can get a double room for the discounted rate of $89 if you stay here two or more nights. That also includes a complimentary daily breakfast and the free use of our health club.

Guest That's a good deal. I'd like to stay at your hotel this Friday and Saturday night.

Reservation Clerk Excellent. [2] May I please have your name, ma'am?

Guest My name is Irene Sellers.

Reservation Clerk [3] Could you spell that, please?

Guest Sure. It's I-R-E-N-E S-E-L-L-E-R-S.

Key Expressions

1 You can get a double room for the discounted rate of $89 if you stay here two or more nights.

이곳에서 이틀 이상 숙박하시면 할인된 요금인 89달러에 더블룸을 이용하실 수 있습니다.

이틀 이상을 숙박하는 손님에게는 할인된 요금에 방을 제공하고 있다는 뜻이다. 어떤 조건을 만족하면 할인이 적용되는지 설명할 때는 if를 사용할 수 있다.

The special price will be applied if you book a room online   온라인으로 방을 예약하시면 특가가 적용될 것입니다.

2 May I please have your name?   성함이 어떻게 되십니까?

May I (please) have ~?는 손님에게 어떤 것을 정중하게 요청할 때 사용할 수 있다. 조동사 may를 can이나 could로 대신할 수 있다.

Could you tell me your name, please?   성함을 말씀해 주시겠습니까?

3 Could you spell that, please?   철자를 불러 주시겠습니까?

이름이나 주소 등과 같은 단어의 철자를 묻는 표현이다. 모르는 이름이거나, 발음은 같아도 여러 개의 철자로 쓰이는 단어의 철자를 확인할 때 사용한다.

How do you spell your last name?   성의 철자가 어떻게 되십니까?

💡 Useful Phrases

무엇을 확인해 보겠다고 하는 표현

Let me check.   확인해 보겠습니다.

Let me check our reservations.   저희의 예약 현황을 확인해 보겠습니다.

Let me check it for you.   그것을 확인해 드리겠습니다.

Basic Drills

 주어진 문장에 어울리는 대답을 고르세요.

1 We also have a special promotional offer this weekend.

2 Do you have any rooms available?

3 That includes a complimentary daily breakfast and the free use of our health club.

ⓐ Let me check.

ⓑ Could you tell me about it?

ⓒ That's a good deal.

 괄호 안의 말을 순서대로 배열하여 주어진 의미를 영어로 표현하세요.

1 이곳에서 이틀 이상 숙박하시면 할인된 요금인 89달러에 더블룸을 이용하실 수 있습니다.
(a double room / two or more nights / for the discounted rate / you can get / of $89 / if you stay here)

➡ ______________________________________

2 성함이 어떻게 되십니까? (have / your name / I / may / please)

➡ ______________________________________

3 철자를 불러 주시겠습니까? (you / spell / please / could / that)

➡ ______________________________________

Buildup Activities 대화를 듣고 빈칸을 채운 후 주어진 질문에 답하세요.

Guest	Good morning. I tried to book a room online but couldn't. I want to get a room for this weekend. Are there any ______________________?
Reservation Clerk	Let me see . . . Yes, we still have a few rooms available. And we're offering a special ______________ this weekend.
Guest	Is that so? What is it?
Reservation Clerk	If you stay here for two or more nights, you can get a double room for only $89. That's ______________ the normal rate. It also comes with a free daily breakfast and free parking.
Guest	What a great ______________. I'd like a double room for this Saturday and Sunday ______________, please.
Reservation Clerk	Great. Could you please tell me your name, sir?
Guest	My name is Jason Hampton.
Reservation Clerk	I'm sorry, but how do you ______________ your last name?
Guest	It's H-A-M-P-T-O-N.

🎧 02-03

1 How much is the discount on the room?
ⓐ 25% off　　ⓑ 40% off　　ⓒ 50% off

2 What kind of room does Mr. Hampton reserve?
ⓐ a single room　　ⓑ a double room　　ⓒ a suite

Conversation II 

다음 대화를 듣고 파트너와 함께 대화를 연습해 보세요.

🎧 02-04

Changing Reservations

Reservation Clerk Royal Hotel. This is Cindy speaking. What can I do for you?

Guest Hello. I have a reservation, but I have to change it. My name is Mark Conner, and my reservation is for tomorrow.

Reservation Clerk I'm sorry, but [1]could you please repeat your name? [2]I think we have a bad connection.

Guest Of course. My name is Mark Conner. My reservation number is RH092-932.

Reservation Clerk Thank you, Mr. Conner. [3]How would you like to change your reservation?

Guest I need to stay at your hotel for two extra days. I will be there from Thursday, April 10, until Tuesday, April 15.

Reservation Clerk That's no problem, Mr. Conner. I just changed it for you. Do you require any more assistance?

Guest No, that's everything. Thank you for your help.

Key Expressions

1 Could you please repeat your name?   성함을 다시 말씀해 주시겠습니까?

Could you (please) repeat ~?는 '~을 다시 말씀해 주시겠습니까?'라는 의미로, 손님이 한 말을 미처 듣지 못했거나, 듣기는 했지만 확인이 필요할 때 사용한다. '반복하다'라는 뜻의 동사 repeat 대신 say again을 사용할 수도 있다.

Can [Could] you say that again, please?   그것을 다시 말씀해 주시겠습니까?

2 I think we have a bad connection.   연결 상태가 나쁜 것 같습니다.

연결 상태가 좋지 않아 손님과 전화 통화 중에 소리가 잘 들리지 않을 때 사용하는 표현이다.

I am sorry, but I can't hear you very well.   죄송하지만, 잘 들리지 않습니다.
You are breaking up, sir [ma'am].   통화가 끊깁니다, 손님.
This is a bad connection.   연결 상태가 나쁩니다.

3 How would you like to change your reservation?   예약을 어떻게 변경해 드릴까요?

예약 내용을 변경하고 싶다는 손님에게 어떻게 변경하고 싶은지 묻는 표현이다.

How do you want to change your reservation?   예약을 어떻게 변경하고 싶으십니까?
What would you like to change?   무엇을 변경하고 싶으십니까?
What change would you like to make?   어떤 변경을 하고 싶으십니까?

💡 Useful Phrases

That's no problem.   문제 없습니다. [물론입니다.]

= That is not a problem.   = Of course.   = Certainly.   = Sure.

Basic Drills

A 주어진 문장에 어울리는 대답을 고르세요.

1 How would you like to change your
reservation?

2 What can I do for you?

3 My name is Mark Conner, and my
reservation is for tomorrow.

ⓐ I have a reservation, but I have to change
it.

ⓑ I'm sorry, but could you please repeat
your name?

ⓒ I need to stay at your hotel for two extra
days.

B 괄호 안의 말을 순서대로 배열하여 주어진 의미를 영어로 표현하세요.

1 성함을 다시 말씀해 주시겠습니까? (please / could / your name / repeat / you)

→ ....

2 연결 상태가 나쁜 것 같습니다. (I / a bad connection / we / think / have)

→ ....

3 예약을 어떻게 변경해 드릴까요? (would you / your reservation / how / change / like to)

→ ....

Buildup Activities   대화를 듣고 빈칸을 채운 후 주어진 질문에 답하세요.

Reservation Clerk	Royal Hotel. Tom ________________________. May I help you?
Guest	Hello. I need to ________________________ my reservation. I'm Susan Daley, and I have a reservation for this Thursday.
Reservation Clerk	I'm sorry, but could you please tell me your name again? There was some static ________________________.
Guest	Of course. My name is Susan Daley. My reservation ________________________ is PTR59-087.
Reservation Clerk	Thank you very much, Ms. Daley. What change would you like to ________________________?
Guest	I'm supposed to ________________________ on Thursday, but I can't go there until this Friday. I will stay at your hotel from Friday until next Monday morning.
Reservation Clerk	I changed your reservation, Ms. Daley. Do you need anything else this morning?
Guest	No, thank you. I appreciate your assistance.

⌂ 02-05

1 **What does the reservation clerk ask Ms. Daley to do?**

ⓐ repeat her name   ⓑ provide her address   ⓒ spell her name

2 **When will Ms. Daley check in?**

ⓐ on Thursday   ⓑ on Friday   ⓒ on Monday

A 〈보기〉에서 적절한 말을 찾아 각 그림의 상황에 맞는 대화를 완성하세요.

보기

We're offering double rooms for only $100 if you stay for at least two nights.

Of course. It's G-E-O-R-G-E S-C-H-M-I-D-T.

Could you let me know your name, please?

1

Can you tell me about the special offer?

2

My name is George Schmidt.

3

Could you please spell your name for me?

B 주어진 세 가지 상황을 이용하여 파트너와 함께 각 상황에 맞는 대화를 연습해 보세요.

Situation	ⓐ	ⓑ	ⓒ
1	a 30% discount	a tour of the city	from Saturday to Tuesday
2	half off	free parking	for four days starting this Wednesday
3	a discount of 20%	50% off a rental car	from the 10th to the 15th

Reservation Clerk	We also have a special promotional offer this weekend.
Guest	Really? Could you tell me about it?
Reservation Clerk	Sure. You can get ⓐ __________ if you stay here two or more nights. That also includes a complimentary daily breakfast and ⓑ __________.
Guest	That's a good deal. I'd like to stay at your hotel ⓒ __________.

Job Simulation II

A 〈보기〉에서 적절한 말을 찾아 각 그림의 상황에 맞는 대화를 완성하세요.

보기

| Let me repeat my name then. | I want to extend my stay by four days. | Could you say your name one more time? |

1

2

It's very hard to hear you.

3

What change would you like to make to your reservation?

B 주어진 세 가지 상황을 이용하여 파트너와 함께 각 상황에 맞는 대화를 연습해 보세요.

Situation	ⓐ	ⓑ
1	say your name one more time	a bit longer
2	say your name more slowly	longer than I had planned
3	speak a little more loudly	for two fewer days than I had planned

Reservation Clerk   I'm sorry, but could you please ⓐ ....? I think we have a bad connection.

Guest   Of course. My name is Mark Conner. My reservation number is RH092-932.

Reservation Clerk   Thank you, Mr. Conner. How would you like to change your reservation?

Guest   I need to stay at your hotel ⓑ .... I will be there from Thursday, April 10, until Tuesday, April 15.

🎧 02-06

Various Types of Hotel Rooms

Most hotels have a wide variety of rooms. One way they differ is by the beds in the rooms. A single room has one single bed [1]while a double room has one double bed or one king-sized bed. A twin room has two single beds, and a triple room has three single beds or one double bed and a single bed. An *ondol* room lacks a bed. Instead, guests sleep on mats on the floor, but the floor is heated. There are different types of rooms, too. Two adjoining rooms are next to each other without a door between them, but two connecting rooms have a door between them. Handicapped rooms are for people with physical disabilities. Smoking is not permitted in nonsmoking rooms. Long-term guest rooms are for people who [2]intend to stay for a month or longer. Hotel rooms can be different sizes as well. Most rooms are standard sized. But superior and deluxe rooms have a larger amount of space and may have separate seating areas. Suites usually have two or more separate rooms.

Words & Phrases

mat a thin piece of fabric set on the floor **adjoining** beside; next to **physical disability** a limitation one has because of one's body
long-term lasting a long time **deluxe** luxurious

Basic Grammar

1 '대조'를 나타내는 접속사 while

while은 '~인 반면에', '~이지만'이라는 대조의 뜻을 나타내는 접속사로, 두 대상의 차이를 보여 준다.

This room has a tub while the one right next to it has a shower booth.   바로 옆 방에는 샤워 부스가 있는 반면에 이 방에는 욕조가 있다.

While the restaurant is open from 7:00 AM to 10:00 PM, room service is available 24 hours a day.
레스토랑은 오전 7시부터 오후 10시까지 문을 열지만, 룸서비스는 24시간 이용 가능합니다.

2 intend to V   ~할 작정이다, ~하려고 생각하다

동사 intend는 to부정사를 목적어로 취하여 '~할 작정이다', '~하려고 생각하다'라는 뜻을 나타낸다. 비슷한 의미로 plan to V (~할 계획이다) 등이 있다.

The couple intended to stay in a family room.   그 부부는 패밀리룸에 묵을 작정이었다.
I am planning to check out late.   나는 체크아웃을 늦게 할 계획이다.

예약했는데 방이 없다는 게 말이 되나요?

호텔 프런트 데스크 직원이 방이 없다는 이유로 예약 손님을 돌려보냅니다. 아니, 예약한 손님을 돌려보내다니. 이게 무슨 영화의 한 장면인가요? 안타깝게도 이것은 현실입니다. 호텔이 보유한 객실 수를 초과해서 예약을 받기 때문에 벌어지는 일인데요. 그렇다면 호텔은 어째서 객실 수보다 더 많은 손님을 받는 '초과 예약(overbooking)'을 하는 것일까요? 이유는 간단합니다. 막판에 예약을 취소하거나 예약만 하고 실제로는 호텔에 오지 않는 손님에 대비해 손님을 더 받아 두는 것이지요. 하지만 예측이 언제나 맞아떨어지는 것은 아니어서, 때때로 손님을 돌려보내는 '턴어웨이(turn away)'를 하는 경우도 생깁니다. 이때 호텔측은 이런 손님들을 위해 근처 호텔에서 객실을 구해 주지요.

Check-in Service

UNIT 03

다음은 체크인 시 볼 수 있는 호텔의 물품입니다. 각 물품의 이름을 아래에서 찾아 써 보세요.

1 ______ 2 ______ 3 ______ 4 ______

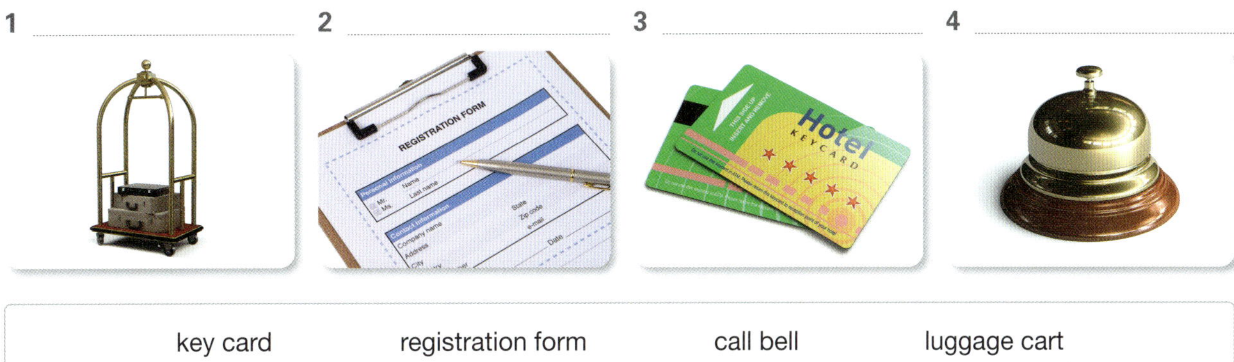

| key card | registration form | call bell | luggage cart |

Vocabulary

주어진 단어와 어울리는 의미를 고르세요.

1 in luck   •   • ⓐ to like one thing more than another

2 prefer   •   • ⓑ a place of interest to visit or look at

3 fill out   •   • ⓒ to enter onto a computer

4 sight   •   • ⓓ lucky; fortunate

5 put into   •   • ⓔ to write some information on a form

Warmup Listening

문장을 듣고 그에 맞는 대답을 고르세요.

1 ⓐ Yes, that's correct.   ⓑ Yes, I checked in two days ago.

2 ⓐ That sounds great to me.   ⓑ I'd like a nonsmoking room.

3 ⓐ Yes, I filled out the form.   ⓑ Here's my passport.

🎧 03-01

다음 대화를 듣고 파트너와 함께 대화를 연습해 보세요.

🎧 03-02

Check-in Service for Reservations Made on a Website

Guest	Good afternoon. I'd like to check in, please.
Front Desk Agent	Good afternoon, ma'am. [1]Do you have a reservation?
Guest	Yes, I do. I made a reservation on your website one week ago. Here is my reservation number.
Front Desk Agent	Thank you very much. Let me put it into the computer . . . Ah, yes, welcome to the Royal Hotel, Ms. Sanderson. [2]You'll be staying with us in a deluxe room for three nights, right?
Guest	Yes, that's correct.
Front Desk Agent	Could I please have your passport and a credit card?
Guest	Here you are.
Front Desk Agent	Thank you. [3]Would you prefer a smoking or nonsmoking room?
Guest	I'd like a nonsmoking room, please.

Key Expressions

1 Do you have a reservation?　예약하셨습니까?

체크인을 하려는 손님에게 예약을 했는지 묻는 말이다. reserve나 make a reservation도 '예약하다'라는 뜻으로 사용할 수 있다.

Do you have a reservation with us?　저희 호텔에 예약하셨습니까?
Did you reserve a hotel room?　호텔 객실을 예약하셨습니까?
Did you make a reservation?　예약하셨습니까?

2 You'll be staying with us in a deluxe room for three nights, right?
손님은 저희 호텔 디럭스룸에서 3일 동안 숙박하실 예정이시지요?

체크인 전에 예약 내용을 손님에게 다시 한번 확인시켜 주는 표현으로, 손님이 예약한 객실의 유형, 숙박 기간, 그리고 흡연·가능 여부 등을 언급할 수 있다.

I see that you will be staying here for a week. Is that correct?　여기서 일주일 동안 숙박하실 예정이십니다. 맞으시지요?
You reserved a family room from the 27th to the 30th.　27일부터 30일까지 패밀리룸을 예약하셨습니다.
Would you prefer a smoking or nonsmoking room?　흡연실과 금연실 중 어느 것을 원하십니까?

3 Would you prefer a smoking or nonsmoking room?　흡연실과 금연실 중 어느 것을 원하십니까?

흡연실과 금연실 중 어떤 객실을 원하는지 묻는 말이다. 둘 중 어느 것을 원하는지 묻는 질문은 Would you prefer A or B?나 Which do you prefer [like], A or B?로 나타낼 수 있다.

Which do you prefer, an ocean or garden view?　해변 전망과 정원 전망 중 어느 것을 원하십니까?
Do you want coffee or tea with your breakfast?　조식과 함께 커피와 차 중 어느 것을 드시겠습니까?

💡 Useful Phrases

Here you are.　여기 있어요.

= Here you go.　　　　= Here it is.　　　　= Here they are. (건네는 물건이 두 개 이상일 때)

Basic Drills

A 주어진 문장에 어울리는 대답을 고르세요.

1 I'd like to check in, please.   •   • ⓐ Yes, that's correct.

2 Would you prefer a smoking or   •   • ⓑ Do you have a reservation?
nonsmoking room?

3 You'll be staying with us in a deluxe   •   • ⓒ I'd like a nonsmoking room, please.
room for three nights, right?

B 괄호 안의 말을 순서대로 배열하여 주어진 의미를 영어로 표현하세요.

1 예약하셨습니까? (you / a reservation / do / have)

→ ____

2 손님은 저희 호텔 디럭스룸에서 3일 동안 숙박하실 예정이시지요?
(you'll / right / for three nights / with us / in a deluxe room / be staying)

→ ____

3 흡연실과 금연실 중 어느 것을 원하십니까? (would you / or / a smoking / nonsmoking room / prefer)

→ ____

Buildup Activities 대화를 듣고 빈칸을 채운 후 주어진 질문에 답하세요.

Guest	Good evening. I would like a room, please.
Front Desk Agent	Hello, sir. Do you have a ________________ here?
Guest	Yes, I do. I booked a room ________________ last night. Here is my information.
Front Desk Agent	Thank you. Let me ________________ everything . . . Welcome to the Royal Hotel, Mr. Yamagata. You reserved a ________________ room for four nights. Is that correct?
Guest	Yes, it is.
Front Desk Agent	May I please see your ________________ and a credit card?
Guest	I have them right here.
Front Desk Agent	Thank you. Would you like a smoking or nonsmoking room?
Guest	A ________________ room would be perfect.

⌒ 03-03

1 When did the guest reserve the room?
   ⓐ last week   ⓑ four days ago   ⓒ last night

2 What type of room does the guest request?
   ⓐ a nonsmoking room
   ⓑ a handicapped-access room
   ⓒ a room with an ocean view

다음 대화를 듣고 파트너와 함께 대화를 연습해 보세요.

🎧 03-04

Check-in Service for Walk-ins

Guest	Good evening. I'd like to get a room, please.
Front Desk Agent	Do you have a reservation?
Guest	No, I don't. I wasn't expecting to stay here, but my connecting flight got canceled. So I have to stay here until tomorrow afternoon.
Front Desk Agent	[1]I'm sorry to hear that, sir. Maybe you can visit a few places in the city before you depart. You're in luck today. We still have a couple of rooms available. Would you prefer a single or double room?
Guest	A single room is fine.
Front Desk Agent	All right. [2]May I see some type of picture ID, please? And [3]could you please fill out this registration form?
Guest	No problem. Here's my driver's license. Do you happen to have a pen?
Front Desk Agent	Yes, there's one on the counter.

Key Expressions

1 **I'm sorry to hear that.**　　그런 말을 들으니 유감입니다.

자신의 잘못에 대한 사과가 아니라 손님이 처한 상황에 대한 안타까움을 나타내는 표현이다.

Oh, I am sorry. That is terrible.　　아, 유감입니다. 정말 안타깝군요.

2 **May I see some type of picture ID, please?**　　사진이 있는 신분증을 보여 주시겠습니까?

손님에게 사진이 있는 신분증을 요청하는 표현이다. 조동사 may 대신 can이나 could를 사용할 수도 있다.

Could you show me some kind of picture ID, sir [ma'am]?　　사진이 있는 신분증을 보여 주시겠습니까?
Do you have any picture ID with you?　　사진이 있는 신분증이 있으십니까?

3 **Could you please fill out this registration form?**　　이 등록 양식을 작성해 주시겠습니까?

체크인을 하는 손님에게 호텔 등록 양식을 작성해 달라고 요청할 때 사용할 수 있다. fill out은 '~을 작성하다'라는 뜻으로, fill in으로 대체할 수 있다.

Would you fill in this form, please?　　이 양식을 작성해 주시겠습니까?

💡 Useful Phrases

예약 가능 여부를 안내하는 표현

We still have a couple of rooms available.
아직 이용 가능한 객실 두어 개가 남아 있습니다.

The only room we have available is a suite.
남은 객실은 스위트룸뿐입니다.

I am afraid all our double rooms are reserved.
안타깝지만 모든 더블룸이 예약되었습니다.

We don't have any rooms available.
이용 가능한 객실이 하나도 없습니다.

Basic Drills

A 주어진 문장에 어울리는 대답을 고르세요.

1 I wasn't expecting to stay here, but my connecting flight got canceled.

2 Would you prefer a single or double room?

3 May I see some type of picture ID, please?

ⓐ A single room is fine.

ⓑ I'm sorry to hear that.

ⓒ Here's my driver's license.

B 괄호 안의 말을 순서대로 배열하여 주어진 의미를 영어로 표현하세요.

1 그런 말을 들으니 유감입니다. (hear / I'm / sorry / that / to)

→ ____

2 사진이 있는 신분증을 보여 주시겠습니까? (see / some / picture ID / may I / type of / please)

→ ____

3 이 등록 양식을 작성해 주시겠습니까? (registration form / fill out / could you / please / this)

→ ____

Buildup Activities 대화를 듣고 빈칸을 채운 후 주어진 질문에 답하세요.

Guest	Hello. Can I please get a room?
Front Desk Agent	Did you ______________ a reservation?
Guest	No, I didn't. I am checking in because my connecting flight got ______________. I was scheduled to leave today, but I won't be able to depart until tomorrow evening.
Front Desk Agent	I'm ______________ sorry about that, ma'am. Maybe you can visit a couple of museums before you leave. It's your lucky day. We have one room ______________. Is a single room okay?
Guest	Yes, a ______________ is perfect.
Front Desk Agent	Great. Do you have some form of picture ID? I need you to ______________ this registration form as well.
Guest	Of course. Here is my passport. May I borrow a pen, please?
Front Desk Agent	Yes, here you are.

∩ 03-05

1 What does the front desk agent suggest that the guest do before she leaves?

ⓐ do some shopping　　ⓑ go to some museums　　ⓒ visit the waterfront

2 What does the front desk agent ask the guest for?

ⓐ a pen　　ⓑ a credit card　　ⓒ an ID card

Job Simulation **I**

A 〈보기〉에서 적절한 말을 찾아 각 그림의 상황에 맞는 대화를 완성하세요.

1

2

3

B 주어진 세 가지 상황을 이용하여 파트너와 함께 각 상황에 맞는 대화를 연습해 보세요.

Situation	ⓐ	ⓑ
1	Did you make a reservation?	a double room for one week
2	Did you already book a room?	a suite tonight and tomorrow
3	Did you reserve a room here?	a junior suite for five nights

Front Desk Agent Good afternoon, ma'am. ⓐ _______________________?

Guest Yes, I did. I made a reservation on your website one week ago. Here is my reservation number.

Front Desk Agent Thank you very much. Let me put it into the computer . . . Ah, yes, welcome to the Royal Hotel, Ms. Sanderson. You'll be staying with us in ⓑ _______________________, right?

Guest Yes, that's correct.

Job Simulation Ⅱ

A 〈보기〉에서 적절한 말을 찾아 각 그림의 상황에 맞는 대화를 완성하세요.

보기

Do you have some type of picture ID?	I'm very sorry about your flight, sir.	Can you fill out this registration form, please?

1

My flight was canceled, so I have to stay here tonight.

2

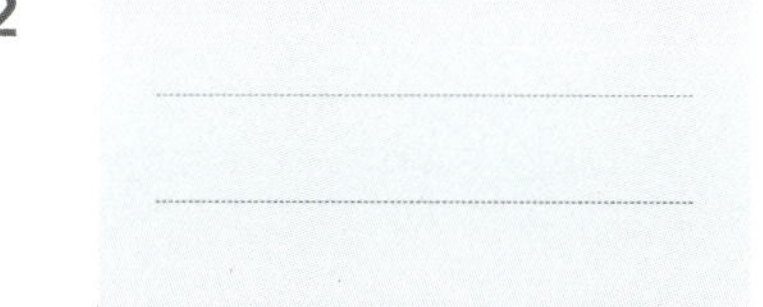

I've got my passport right here.

3

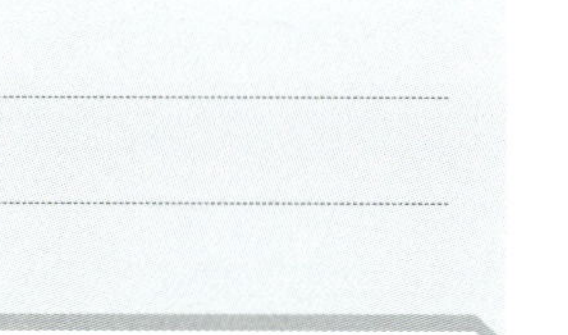

Yes, but I need a pen.

B 주어진 세 가지 상황을 이용하여 파트너와 함께 각 상황에 맞는 대화를 연습해 보세요.

Situation	ⓐ	ⓑ
1	sometime tomorrow	We still have some rooms available
2	tomorrow afternoon	We aren't fully occupied
3	tomorrow at 2:00 PM	We have a few vacancies

Front Desk Agent Do you have a reservation?

Guest No, I don't. My connecting flight got canceled. So I have to stay here until ⓐ ______________.

Front Desk Agent I'm sorry to hear that, sir. Maybe you can visit a few places in the city before you depart. You're in luck today. ⓑ ______________. Would you prefer a single or double room?

Guest A single room is fine.

🎧 03-06

The Front Desk: The Face of a Hotel

For most guests, the first person they speak with at a hotel is someone working at the front desk. So guests often form their initial impressions of hotels by how their interactions at the front desk go. For that reason, the front desk is considered the face of a hotel. People working at the front desk have many responsibilities. They check guests in and out of their rooms. They handle reservation requests, changes, and cancelations. They receive payments from guests. They answer telephone calls and transfer calls to the proper departments. They [1]let housekeeping know when guests are arriving and leaving. They also take care of various problems that guests have with their rooms. Workers at the front desk must be able to multitask. They must also be pleasant and smile all the time [2]since they are constantly representing their hotel.

Words & Phrases

initial first   **impression** a feeling or opinion   **interaction** communication or contact with another person   **handle** to take care of   **proper** correct   **multitask** to do two or more activities at the same time

Basic Grammar

1 사역동사 let

let은 '~하게 하다'라는 뜻으로, 여기에서는 '알다'라는 뜻의 동사원형 know를 목적격 보어로 취하여 '알게 하다'라는 뜻을 나타내고 있다. 다른 사역동사로는 have와 make가 있다

Let the front desk know if you are checking out late.   체크아웃을 늦게 하실 경우 프런트 데스크에 알려 주세요.
Bill let the housekeeper know that he wouldn't need new towels.   빌은 새 수건이 필요하지 않을 것이라고 객실관리 담당자에게 알렸다.

2 '이유'를 나타내는 접속사 since

since는 '~이기 때문에'라고 해석되며, 이유를 나타내는 부사절을 이끈다. 같은 의미의 접속사로는 because, as, for 등이 있다.

The restaurant is currently closed because it is being renovated.   레스토랑은 수리 중이기 때문에 현재 닫혀 있다.
As the connecting flight got canceled, the whole family had to stay at a hotel.
연결편이 취소되었기 때문에 가족 모두가 호텔에 머물러야 했다.

TIPS & TIPS

미스터리 쇼퍼, 당신은 누구인가요?

한 손님이 TV 리모컨에서 배터리를 빼 버리고는 프런트 데스크에 전화해 리모컨 작동이 안 된다고 따집니다. 잠시 후에는 객실에서 나지도 않는 냄새가 난다며 또 따집니다. 대체 이 손님은 뭘 하고 있는 걸까요? 이 손님은 이상한 사람이 아닙니다. 바로 호텔에서 고용한 '미스터리 쇼퍼(mystery shopper)'이지요. 특급 호텔은 항상 고객에게 최고의 서비스를 제공하려고 노력합니다. 그래서 이들을 고용하는 것이지요. 미스터리 쇼퍼는 손님으로 가장해 호텔에 묵으면서 호텔 서비스를 평가합니다. 없던 문제도 만들어 호텔이 어떻게 대처하는지 확인하기도 하고요. 그리고는 호텔에 피드백을 전달하여 실제 고객에게 더 나은 서비스를 제공할 수 있도록 한답니다.

Giving Essential Information about Hotel Services

UNIT 04

다음은 호텔에서 일하는 직원들의 업무입니다. 각 업무에 해당하는 직원을 사진에서 고르세요.

1 escort guests to their rooms and carry their luggage ....

2 check guests in, assign rooms, and check them out ....

3 clean rooms, make beds, and collect guests' laundry ....

4 provide all kinds of information about the hotel and other places ....

ⓐ room maid

ⓑ concierge

ⓒ front desk agent

ⓓ bellman

Vocabulary

주어진 단어와 어울리는 의미를 고르세요.

1 pick up •   • ⓐ to be in a certain place

2 lobby •   • ⓑ the front area of a building

3 escort •   • ⓒ to provide food, an item, or a service for someone

4 be located •   • ⓓ to take a person somewhere

5 serve •   • ⓔ to collect

Warmup Listening

문장을 듣고 그에 맞는 대답을 고르세요.

1 ⓐ You can eat bacon, eggs, and pancakes.　　ⓑ Anytime between 6:00 and 10:00 AM.

2 ⓐ Just dial 1.　　ⓑ Yes, we can dry-clean your suit.

🎧 04-01

3 ⓐ I'll serve you dinner in a moment.　　ⓑ We have a spa and a business center.

다음 대화를 듣고 파트너와 함께 대화를 연습해 보세요.

🎧 04-02

Providing Essential Information about Rooms and Services

Front Desk Agent Here's your room key, Mr. Taylor. Your room is on the fourth floor. You can take the elevator right over there. [1] Just take a left as soon as you get off the elevator.

Guest Thank you. Oh, when is breakfast served here?

Front Desk Agent [2] Our hotel restaurant serves breakfast from 5:00 to 10:30 AM. It's located on the fifteenth floor.

Guest Do I have to pay for it?

Front Desk Agent No, you don't. [3] Your room reservation includes a complimentary breakfast for two each day. So you can enjoy the breakfast buffet for free. Do you have any other questions?

Guest Yes, I have one more. How can I get my clothes cleaned?

Front Desk Agent Dial 0 when you get to your room. Then, you can ask to have someone visit your room to pick up your laundry.

Key Expressions

1 **Just take a left as soon as you get off the elevator.** 엘리베이터에서 내리자마자 좌회전하시면 됩니다.

객실이나 호텔 내 시설의 위치를 설명할 때 사용할 수 있는 표현이다. make a left turn도 '좌회전하다'라는 뜻이다.

Go upstairs to the mezzanine floor and make a right [left] turn. 계단으로 중간층까지 올라가셔서 우회전[좌회전]하세요.

2 **Our hotel restaurant serves breakfast from 5:00 to 10:30 AM.**
저희 호텔 레스토랑은 오전 5시부터 10시 30분까지 조식을 제공합니다.

이 표현은 호텔에서 조식 시간을 안내할 때 사용할 수 있으며, 동사 serve는 '제공하다'라는 의미를 나타낸다.

You can have breakfast between 7:00 and 10:00 AM. 오전 7시에서 오전 10시 사이에 조식을 드실 수 있습니다.
Breakfast is served from 6:30 to 10:00 in the morning. 조식은 오전 6시 30분부터 10시까지 제공됩니다.

3 **Your room reservation includes a complimentary breakfast for two each day.**
손님의 객실 예약에는 매일 2인을 위한 무료 조식이 포함되어 있습니다.

손님이 예약한 객실에는 매일 2인의 무료 조식이 포함되어 있다는 의미로, 형용사 complimentary(무료의)는 free로 대신할 수 있다.

Free breakfast for two people is included in your reservation. 2인의 무료 조식이 손님의 예약에 포함되어 있습니다.

💡 Useful Phrases

층수를 나타내는 표현

층수	미국 영어	영국 영어
3층	third floor	second floor
2층	second floor	first floor
1층	first floor	ground floor

Basic Drills

A 주어진 문장에 어울리는 대답을 고르세요.

1 Do I have to pay for it?   •   • **ⓐ** Dial 0 when you get to your room.

2 How can I get my clothes cleaned?   •   • **ⓑ** Our hotel restaurant serves breakfast from 5:00 to 10:30 AM.

3 When is breakfast served here?   •   • **ⓒ** No, you don't.

B 괄호 안의 말을 순서대로 배열하여 주어진 의미를 영어로 표현하세요.

1 엘리베이터에서 내리자마자 좌회전하시면 됩니다. (you / just / the elevator / as soon as / take a left / get off)

→

2 저희 호텔 레스토랑은 오전 5시부터 10시 30분까지 조식을 제공합니다.
(our / serves / to 10:30 AM / hotel restaurant / from 5:00 / breakfast)

→

3 손님의 객실 예약에는 매일 2인을 위한 무료 조식이 포함되어 있습니다.
(a complimentary breakfast / each day / includes / your / room reservation / for two)

→

Buildup Activities   대화를 듣고 빈칸을 채운 후 주어진 질문에 답하세요.

Front Desk Agent	Here's your key card, Ms. Chin. Your room is on the tenth ________________. You can take the elevator right behind you. All you have to do is turn right once you get off the elevator.
Guest	Thank you. By the way, what time can I have ________________ ?
Front Desk Agent	The hotel restaurant provides breakfast from 5:00 to 11:00 AM. You can find it on the fourth floor.
Guest	________________ is breakfast?
Front Desk Agent	Actually, your room reservation comes with a ________________ breakfast every day. So the breakfast buffet costs nothing. Do you want to know anything else?
Guest	Yes, I have another question. How can I get ________________ ?
Front Desk Agent	Dial 0 from your room telephone. Then, you can ________________ anything from the menu twenty-four hours a day.

🎧 04-03

1 **Where is the guest's room?**
   ⓐ on the fourth floor   **ⓑ** on the tenth floor   **ⓒ** on the fifteenth floor

2 **What does the guest ask the front desk agent about?**
   ⓐ what food is served at breakfast
   ⓑ how to get laundry service
   ⓒ how to order room service

Conversation II 

다음 대화를 듣고 파트너와 함께 대화를 연습해 보세요.

🎧 04-04

Explaining Hotel Facilities and Services

Bellman	Please follow me, ma'am, and I'll escort you to your room.
Guest	Thank you very much.
Bellman	Let me tell you about the hotel's facilities. The restaurant and the bar are located near the lobby. [1]We also have a fitness center, a wellness center, and a swimming pool on the third floor.
Guest	That sounds great. I'll be sure to visit the pool later in the day. What other services does the hotel provide?
Bellman	[2]You can order room service 24 hours a day. There is a business center on the fifth floor, too.
Guest	Thank you very much. I appreciate all the information.
Bellman	It's my pleasure. Here we are. This is your room, ma'am. After you, ma'am . . . Shall I put your bags here?
Guest	Yes, please.
Bellman	Here is your room telephone. [3]Dial 0 if you need anything.

Key Expressions

1 **We also have a fitness center, a wellness center, and a swimming pool on the third floor.**

또한 3층에는 피트니스 센터, 웰니스 센터, 그리고 수영장이 있습니다.

호텔 안에 있는 시설에 관하여 설명할 때는 We have를 사용하여 '~을 가지고 있습니다'라고 말할 수 있으며, There is [are]를 사용하여 '~이 있습니다'라고 표현할 수도 있다.

There is an outdoor pool next to the tennis court.   테니스 코트 옆에 실외 수영장이 있습니다.

2 **You can order room service 24 hours a day.**   24시간 내내 룸서비스를 주문하실 수 있습니다.

룸서비스 이용 가능 시간을 설명할 때 사용할 수 있는 문장으로, between A and B나 from A to B를 사용하여 구체적인 시간을 나타낼 수도 있다.

From 11:00 AM to 11:00 PM, you can order room service.   오전 11시부터 오후 11시까지 룸서비스를 이용하실 수 있습니다.

3 **Dial 0 if you need anything.**   필요한 것이 있으시면 0번으로 전화해 주세요.

객실 내에 비치된 전화기로 0번을 누르면 교환원이나 프런트 데스크로 연결된다는 것을 안내할 때 사용하는 표현이다. 동사 dial 대신 call을 사용할 수도 있다.

Call the front desk in case you need anything.   필요한 것이 있으신 경우 프런트 데스크로 전화해 주세요.

💡 Useful Phrases

Yes, please. 그렇게 해 주세요. [그게 좋겠네요.]

= Sure.   = Why not?   = That would be great.

Basic Drills

A 주어진 문장에 어울리는 대답을 고르세요.

1 We also have a fitness center, a wellness center, and a swimming pool on the third floor.

2 Shall I put your bags here?

3 What other services does the hotel provide?

   ⓐ That sounds great.

   ⓑ Yes, please.

   ⓒ You can order room service 24 hours a day.

B 괄호 안의 말을 순서대로 배열하여 주어진 의미를 영어로 표현하세요.

1 또한 3층에는 피트니스 센터, 웰니스 센터, 그리고 수영장이 있습니다.
(and / we also have / on / a fitness center / a wellness center / a swimming pool / the third floor)

→ ____

2 24시간 내내 룸서비스를 주문하실 수 있습니다. (24 hours / you / a day / room service / can order)

→ ____

3 필요한 것이 있으시면 0번으로 전화해 주세요. (anything / if / you / need / dial 0)

→ ____

Buildup Activities 대화를 듣고 빈칸을 채운 후 주어진 질문에 답하세요.

Bellman Follow me, ma'am. Please allow me to _____________ you to your room.

Guest Thank you so much.

Bellman I'd like to tell you a bit about the hotel's facilities. The restaurant and two bars are located on the second floor. The _____________, the wellness center, and the swimming pool are all on the fifth floor.

Guest That sounds great. I'd like to go to the _____________ for a massage later tonight. What other services does the hotel have?

Bellman It's possible to order room service 24 hours a day. We have a business center on the _____________, too.

Guest Excellent. I appreciate you telling me everything.

Bellman It's my pleasure. Here we are. This is your room, ma'am. After you, ma'am . . . Shall I put _____________ over here?

Guest Yes, that would be perfect.

Bellman Your room telephone is here. _____________ 5 if you require anything.

04-05

1 Where does the guest want to go later?
  ⓐ the swimming pool   ⓑ the wellness center   ⓒ the business center

2 What should the guest do if she needs something?
  ⓐ dial 5 on the room telephone   ⓑ call the bellman   ⓒ speak with a room maid

Job Simulation Ⅰ

〈보기〉에서 적절한 말을 찾아 각 그림의 상황에 맞는 대화를 완성하세요.

보 기

| Take a right when you get out of the elevator. | How much does breakfast cost? | You can get breakfast anytime between 5:00 and 10:00 AM. |

1

How can I get to my room?

2

What time is breakfast available at the restaurant?

3

Your reservation includes a complimentary daily breakfast for two.

주어진 세 가지 상황을 이용하여 파트너와 함께 각 상황에 맞는 대화를 연습해 보세요.

Situation	ⓐ	ⓑ	ⓒ
1	on the second floor	get room service	order something to eat
2	beside the lobby	use the business center	let someone there know you are coming
3	on the top floor	get my suit pressed	ask someone to collect your suit for you

Front Desk Agent Our hotel restaurant serves breakfast from 5:00 to 10:30 AM. It's located ⓐ _____________________. Do you have any other questions?

Guest Yes, I have one more. How can I ⓑ _____________________?

Front Desk Agent Dial 0 when you get to your room. Then, you can ⓒ _____________________.

Job Simulation II

A 〈보기〉에서 적절한 말을 찾아 각 그림의 상황에 맞는 대화를 완성하세요.

All you have to do is dial 0.

You can order room service anytime and also have your laundry done.

The hotel has a fitness center, a spa, and a swimming pool.

1

That sounds wonderful.

2

What other services are available here?

3

What should I do if I need something?

B 주어진 세 가지 상황을 이용하여 파트너와 함께 각 상황에 맞는 대화를 연습해 보세요.

Situation	ⓐ	ⓑ
1	all day and night	on the floor
2	at all hours of the day	next to the bed
3	from 5:00 AM to midnight	on this table

Guest   What other services does the hotel provide?

Bellman   You can order room service ⓐ ________________. There is a business center on the fifth floor, too.

Guest   Thank you. I appreciate all the information.

Bellman   It's my pleasure. Here we are. This is your room, ma'am. After you, ma'am . . . Shall I put your bags ⓑ ________________?

Reading & Listening

다음 지문을 읽고 음성을 들어 보세요.

Services That Hotels Provide

These days, hotels do not just [1]provide rooms for their guests. Instead, they also provide a wide variety of services. Most hotels run 24 hours a day. So guests can order room service and check in any time of the day. And because people do business all around the world, most hotels have business centers. Some of them are even open 24 hours a day. At the front desk, there are multilingual clerks, so they can assist guests from different countries. Express check-in and checkout are also available to speed up the process. In the lobby, the concierge can take care of problems and provide information, and valets park guests' vehicles. There are also usually places to exchange currency and safety deposit boxes for holding valuables. [2]Once guests arrive at their rooms, they can call for laundry service and order room service. Their rooms typically have high-speed Internet access, and guests can get wakeup calls as well. Hotels provide cribs for guests with babies, and many offer babysitting services and have kids' cafés for children to play in.

Words & Phrases

multilingual able to speak three or more languages   **express** very fast and convenient   **valet** a parking attendant at a hotel, restaurant, or similar place   **safety deposit box** a strongbox in which people keep their valuables   **crib** a bed for a baby

Basic Grammar

1 provide A for B   A를 B에게 제공하다

동사 provide는 '제공하다'라는 뜻으로, 전치사 for와 함께 provide A for B의 형식으로 쓰인다. 전치사 for 대신 with가 쓰이는 경우, A와 B의 자리가 바뀌어 provide B with A(B에게 A를 제공하다)가 된다.

Our hotel provides the best service for our guests.   저희 호텔은 손님들에게 최고의 서비스를 제공합니다.
We provide guests with two complimentary bottles of water every day.   저희는 손님들에게 매일 두 병의 생수를 무료로 제공합니다.

2 접속사 once

once는 '일단 ~하면'이라는 뜻의 접속사로, 문장에서 조건의 의미를 나타내는 부사절을 이끈다.

Once the holiday starts, the prices of rooms go up.   일단 휴일이 시작되면 객실 가격이 올라간다.
Once you get off the elevator, you will see the restaurant in front of you.   일단 엘리베이터에서 내리시면 손님 앞에 레스토랑이 보이실 것입니다.

TIPS & TIPS

아기만 봐 주시나요? 저희 개는요?

요새는 여행을 갈 때 아이나 반려 동물을 데리고 가는 사람이 많습니다. 하지만 모처럼 부부가 여행을 와서 오붓하게 둘만의 시간을 보내고 싶은데, 아이는 어떻게 해야 할지 난감할 때가 있습니다. 이런 부부를 위해 호텔에는 아이를 돌봐 주는 서비스가 있습니다. 호텔 직원이 아이를 돌봐 주고, 아이와 놀아 주고, 아이에게 밥까지 챙겨 줍니다. 심지어 공부를 봐 주기도 한다고 하네요. 비용은 시간당 또는 일당으로 지불할 수 있습니다. 뿐만 아니라 요즘은 반려 동물을 맡아 주는 서비스도 생겼습니다. 먹이고 놀아 주는 것도 부족해서 산책까지 시켜 준다니 많은 부부가 안심하고 둘만의 시간을 보낼 수 있겠네요.

Giving Local Information

Warmup

다음은 어떤 지역의 관광 지도입니다. 공항에서 호텔까지의 교통 수단별 소요 시간 및 요금을 보고 아래 빈칸을 채워 보세요.

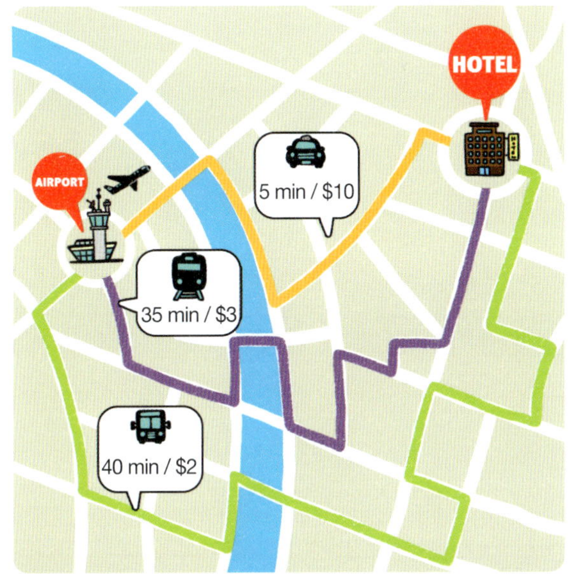

1 The fastest way to get to the hotel is by ....

2 The cheapest way to go to the hotel is by ....

3 The bus takes five minutes longer than the ....

taxi	subway	bus

Vocabulary   주어진 단어와 어울리는 의미를 고르세요.

1 heart •   • ⓐ to recommend
2 highly •   • ⓑ the middle or center of a place
3 suggest •   • ⓒ instructions
4 purchase •   • ⓓ to buy
5 directions •   • ⓔ strongly

Warmup Listening   문장을 듣고 그에 맞는 대답을 고르세요.

1 ⓐ You should take a taxi.   ⓑ The taxi stand is over there.

2 ⓐ It costs $10.   ⓑ You can buy one at the gift shop.

3 ⓐ How about visiting the museum?   ⓑ We're going to the museum soon.

Coneirge I

다음 대화를 듣고 파트너와 함께 대화를 연습해 보세요.

🎧 05-02

Giving Advice about Local Travel

Guest Good morning. Could you give me some assistance, please?

Concierge Of course. What do you need help with?

Guest I'd like to take my family downtown to see the sights. What's the best way to get there?

Concierge The easiest way is to take a taxi. [1]There is a taxi stand located right in front of the hotel. [2]It usually costs around 25 euros to get to the heart of downtown.

Guest How about taking a tram? Does the tram stop near here?

Concierge Yes. There's a tram stop down by the corner. I've got a schedule for the tram right here. But [3]you need to purchase a tram card for each member of your family.

Guest Where can I do that?

Concierge You can get the cards you need at the hotel's gift shop. Follow me. I'll take you there.

Key Expressions

1 **There is a taxi stand located right in front of the hotel.**   호텔 바로 앞에 택시 승강장이 있습니다.

손님에게 어디에서 택시와 같은 교통 수단을 이용할 수 있는지 설명하는 문장이다. in front of(~ 앞에) 외에도 next to(~ 옆에), behind(~ 뒤에), across(~ 건너편에) 등을 사용하여 위치를 표현할 수 있다.

You can catch a cab right next to the fountain.   분수대 바로 옆에서 택시를 잡으실 수 있습니다.
There are many buses across from the hotel.   호텔 건너편에 많은 버스가 있습니다.

2 **It usually costs around 25 euros to get to the heart of downtown.**   시내 중심가까지 가는데 보통 약 25유로가 듭니다.

목적지까지 교통비가 얼마나 드는지 설명하는 표현이다. '(비용이) 들다'라는 의미는 동사 cost 대신 be동사를 사용해 표현할 수도 있다.

It will be around 3,000 yen to go to the airport from here.   여기서 공항까지 가는데 약 3,000엔이 들 것입니다.

3 **You need to purchase a tram card for each member of your family.**   가족 수대로 트램 카드를 구매하셔야 합니다.

트램과 같은 특정 교통 수단을 어떻게 이용하는지 설명하는 문장이다. 동사 purchase 대신 get과 buy도 '구매하다'라는 뜻으로 사용할 수 있다.

You have to buy a ticket to the museum.   박물관 입장권을 구매하셔야 합니다.

💡 Useful Phrases

Could you give me some assistance, please?   도와 주시겠어요?

= Can you help me, please?

= Would you give me a hand?

= Could you help me with something, please?

= Would you do me a favor?

Basic Drills

A 주어진 문장에 어울리는 대답을 고르세요.

1 You need to purchase a tram card for each member of your family.

2 Does the tram stop near here?

3 Could you give me some assistance, please?

ⓐ Where can I do that?

ⓑ What do you need help with?

ⓒ Yes. There's a tram stop down by the corner.

B 괄호 안의 말을 순서대로 배열하여 주어진 의미를 영어로 표현하세요.

1 호텔 바로 앞에 택시 승강장이 있습니다. (a taxi stand / the hotel / right / located / there is / in front of)

→

2 시내 중심가까지 가는데 보통 약 25유로가 듭니다.
(costs / the heart of downtown / it / around 25 euros / to get / to / usually)

→

3 가족 수대로 트램 카드를 구매하셔야 합니다. (your family / you need to / for / each member of / purchase / a tram card)

→

Buildup Activities 대화를 듣고 빈칸을 채운 후 주어진 질문에 답하세요.

Guest	Good morning. Can you help me, please?
Concierge	______________________. What can I assist you with?
Guest	I'd like to take my family to the ______________ district to go sightseeing. How should we go there?
Concierge	The fastest way is by taking a rideshare. You can have a car ______________ in front of the hotel. It should cost about 30 euros to get to that part of town.
Guest	What about the bus? Is there a ______________ nearby?
Concierge	Yes, there is. There's a bus stop one block from here. I've got a schedule for the bus here. But you need to purchase a transportation card for everyone in your family.
Guest	______________ can I buy them?
Concierge	The hotel's ______________ sells them. Please follow me. I'll take you there.

🎧 05-03

1 Where does the guest want to go?

ⓐ the waterfront

ⓑ the theater district

ⓒ downtown

2 What can the guest use a transportation card to take?

ⓐ the tram

ⓑ the subway

ⓒ the bus

Conversation II

다음 대화를 듣고 파트너와 함께 대화를 연습해 보세요.

🎧 05-04

Advising Guests on Visitor Attractions

Guest	I'd like to see the sights in the city this morning. Where do you suggest that I go?
Concierge	Do you enjoy museums? The city has several good museums. [1]I highly recommend the museum of natural history.
Guest	That sounds interesting. What else should I do?
Concierge	As you may know, the city has several sites of historical interest. A tour of several palaces and temples will leave from this hotel in about twenty minutes. It lasts around six hours.
Guest	I don't have that much time. I need to attend a business meeting in the afternoon.
Concierge	In that case, [2]why don't you go to the museum of natural history? After that, you can visit the art gallery next to it.
Guest	Okay. I think I'll do that. How do I get there?
Concierge	[3]Let me write the address and directions for you.

Key Expressions

1 I highly recommend the museum of natural history.   저는 자연사 박물관을 강력히 추천합니다.

호텔에 머무는 손님에게 주변 관광지를 추천할 때 사용한다. 부사 highly 대신 strongly를 쓸 수도 있다.

I'm sure you'd enjoy a ferry ride around the bay.   만 주변을 도는 페리를 좋아하실 겁니다.

2 Why don't you go to the museum of natural history?   자연사 박물관에 가는 것이 어떠십니까?

Why don't you ~?는 '~하는 것이 어떠십니까?'라는 뜻으로, 상대에게 무엇을 제안할 때 사용하는 표현이다. How [What] about ~? 을 사용하여 제안할 수도 있다.

How [What] about the Calgary Art Museum?   캘거리 미술관은 어떠십니까?

3 Let me write the address and directions for you.   제가 주소와 가는 방법을 적어 드리겠습니다.

손님이 가고자 하는 장소의 주소와 가는 방법을 알려 주겠다고 제안하는 표현이다. Let me ~ (제가 ~하겠습니다) 대신에 I can ~ for you (제가 ~해 드릴 수 있습니다)를 사용할 수도 있다.

Let me get a city map for you.   제가 시내 지도를 드리겠습니다.
I can write down the directions for you.   제가 가는 방법을 적어 드릴 수 있습니다.

 **Useful Phrases**

Do you enjoy museums?   박물관을 좋아하십니까?

= Do you like museums?	= Are you interested in museums?
= Do you fancy museums?	= Are you a fan of museums?

Basic Drills

A 주어진 문장에 어울리는 대답을 고르세요.

1 How do I get there?   •   • **ⓐ** I don't have that much time.

2 It lasts around six hours.   •   • **ⓑ** I highly recommend the museum of natural history.

3 Where do you suggest that I go?   •   • **ⓒ** Let me write the address and directions for you.

B 괄호 안의 말을 순서대로 배열하여 주어진 의미를 영어로 표현하세요.

1 저는 자연사 박물관을 강력히 추천합니다. (highly / the museum / I / recommend / of natural history)

➡ ____

2 자연사 박물관에 가는 것이 어떠십니까? (go to / the museum / why don't you / of natural history)

➡ ____

3 제가 주소와 가는 방법을 적어 드리겠습니다. (for you / the address / write / let me / and directions)

➡ ____

Buildup Activities   대화를 듣고 빈칸을 채운 후 주어진 질문에 답하세요.

Guest	I'd like to go _____________ downtown today. Where do you think I should go?
Concierge	What about _____________? The city has several good ones. I strongly suggest that you visit the national art gallery.
Guest	That sounds good. What else should I check out?
Concierge	As you may know, this is a very _____________ with many historical sites. A tour of some ancient ruins and castles is leaving from here in ten minutes. It lasts all day.
Guest	I don't have time for that. I need to _____________ at three.
Concierge	I see. Then why don't you go to the national art gallery? After that, you can go to your _____________ meeting from there.
Guest	Okay. Thanks for the suggestion. How can I get there?
Concierge	I'll show you where it is on _____________.

🎧 05-05

1 What does the concierge say about the city?

  ⓐ It is old.

  ⓑ It has many museums.

  ⓒ It is expensive.

2 What will the guest do at three?

  ⓐ go on a tour

  ⓑ meet a client

  ⓒ go to an art gallery

A 〈보기〉에서 적절한 말을 찾아 각 그림의 상황에 맞는 대화를 완성하세요.

보기

| How much is it to go downtown by taxi? | You need to buy a tram card for everyone taking it. | There are always taxis at the hotel's front door. |

1

Where can I take a taxi?

2

It costs about 15 euros to get downtown from here.

3

How can I pay for the tram?

B 주어진 세 가지 상황을 이용하여 파트너와 함께 각 상황에 맞는 대화를 연습해 보세요.

Situation	ⓐ	ⓑ	ⓒ
1	the downtown area	around the corner	the front desk
2	the middle of downtown	two blocks from here	the convenience store in the lobby
3	where you're going	across the street	the counter by the front desk

Concierge The easiest way is to take a taxi. It usually costs around 25 euros to get to ⓐ __________.

Guest How about taking a tram? Does the tram stop near here?

Concierge Yes. There's a tram stop ⓑ __________. But you need to purchase a tram card for each member of your family. You can do that at ⓒ __________.

Job Simulation II

A 〈보기〉에서 적절한 말을 찾아 각 그림의 상황에 맞는 대화를 완성하세요.

Can you tell me how to get there?

I strongly believe you should visit the city's museum.

Why don't you go to the local art gallery?

1

Where do you think I should go?

2

Okay. I think I will go there.

3

Sure. I can write the address and directions down for you.

B 주어진 세 가지 상황을 이용하여 파트너와 함께 각 상황에 맞는 대화를 연습해 보세요.

Situation	ⓐ	ⓑ
1	fashion museum	five minutes from now
2	dinosaur museum	at 11:00 AM
3	museum of local history	in a few minutes

Guest   I'd like to see the sights in the city this morning. Where do you suggest that I go?

Concierge   Do you enjoy museums? I highly recommend the ⓐ _______________.

Guest   That sounds interesting. What else should I do?

Concierge   As you may know, the city has several sites of historical interest. A tour of several palaces and temples will leave from this hotel ⓑ _______________. It lasts around six hours.

다음 지문을 읽고 음성을 들어 보세요.

🎧 05 - 06

The Concierge: The Representative of a Hotel

One of the most important people at a hotel is the concierge. [1]It is the concierge's job to make sure that guests have everything they need. The concierge frequently provides assistance with reservations. These can be for restaurants, trains, and planes. The concierge also gets things that guests need. If a guest needs to send a letter or mail a package, the concierge can handle it. If a guest needs a new pair of earrings, the concierge can get those as well. The concierge often speaks at least one foreign language and knows the city very well. So the concierge is aware of the best restaurants and shopping areas and the most interesting museums, galleries, and other sightseeing places. The concierge does everything with a smile on his or her face, too. [2]By being pleasant, courteous, and knowledgeable, the concierge can be a good representative of the hotel.

Words & Phrases

pair two of the same kind of item　**be aware of** to know about　**gallery** a place where art is displayed or sold　**pleasant** nice; kind
courteous having good manners; polite

Basic Grammar

1　It ~ to V 진주어 · 가주어 구문

이 구문은 가짜 주어 It으로 시작하고 진짜 주어인 to부정사를 뒤로 빼는 구문으로서, 보통 주어가 길고 복잡할 때 주어를 뒤로 보내기 위해 사용한다.

It is easier to take the shuttle bus to the museum than the train.　박물관까지 셔틀 버스를 타는 것이 기차를 타는 것보다 편합니다.
It is possible to request a wakeup call anytime you want.　언제든지 모닝콜을 신청하시는 것이 가능합니다.

2　by –ing　～함으로써

'～에 의하여'라는 뜻의 전치사 by와 '～하는 것'이라는 뜻의 동명사(–ing)가 짝을 이루어 '～하는 것에 의하여' 혹은 '～함으로써'라는 의미를 나타낸다.

Let us know if you need anything by calling the front desk.　필요한 것이 있으시면 프런트 데스크에 전화하셔서 저희에게 알려 주십시오.
You can get a room for a discounted rate by using this coupon.　이 쿠폰을 사용함으로써 할인된 요금으로 객실을 이용하실 수 있습니다.

TIPS & TIPS

트램이 뭐예요?

유럽이나 북아메리카를 방문하는 사람들은 특이한 교통 수단을 보게 될 것입니다. 바로 '트램(tram)'인데요, 트램은 streetcar나 trolley라고도 불립니다. 기차처럼 정해진 레일 위를 달리지만, 그 레일이 도로에 설치되어 있다는 것이 독특한 점입니다. 다른 차들이 지나다니는 도로를 함께 사용해야 하니 트램 운전기사는 매우 조심해서 운전해야 합니다. 트램이 특별한 이유는 다른 대중 교통 수단에 비해 흔하지 않다는 점도 있지만, 전기로 움직여서 조용하고 친환경적이라는 점에 있을지도 모릅니다. 기회가 된다면 꼭 타보세요. 특히나 샌프란시스코처럼 언덕이 많은 곳에서 트램을 타는 것은 흔치 않은 경험이 될 테니까요.

UNIT 06
Restaurant & Bar Service

다음은 호텔 레스토랑의 메뉴판입니다. 각 코스에 해당하는 메뉴를 아래에서 두 가지씩 찾아 써 보세요.

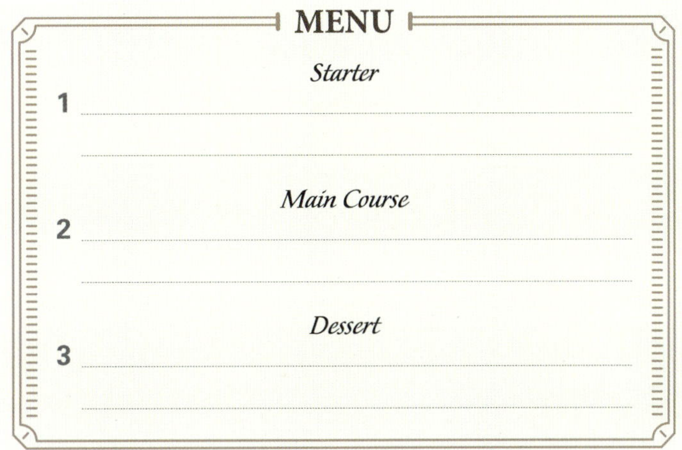

- ⓐ Crispy Shrimp with Lemon Sauce
- ⓑ Grilled Salmon with Asparagus
- ⓒ Caesar Salad with Chicken
- ⓓ Homemade Seasonal Sorbet
- ⓔ Chocolate Mousse
- ⓕ Roasted Lamb Ribs with Garlic

Vocabulary 주어진 단어와 어울리는 의미를 고르세요.

1 a la carte	•	• ⓐ to choose; to select
2 draft	•	• ⓑ well known
3 familiar	•	• ⓒ many types of
4 decide	•	• ⓓ with a separate price for each item on the menu
5 all kinds of	•	• ⓔ taken from a cask or barrel, not a bottle

Warmup Listening 문장을 듣고 그에 맞는 대답을 고르세요.

1 ⓐ I have two guests.　　　ⓑ Yes, that's correct.

2 ⓐ You need to pay extra then.　　　ⓑ Yes, may I take your order, please?

3 ⓐ I'm drinking a beer now.　　　ⓑ I'll have a soda.

🎧 06-01

Conversation **I**

다음 대화를 듣고 파트너와 함께 대화를 연습해 보세요.

🎧 06-02

Breakfast at the Restaurant

Waiter Good morning, ma'am. Welcome to the Skyview restaurant. [1]Would you like to have the breakfast buffet or see a menu?

Guest Good morning. I'm sorry, but I haven't decided yet.

Waiter [2]Are you a guest at the hotel?

Guest Yes, I am. Why do you ask?

Waiter Hotel guests can enjoy a complimentary breakfast buffet. There are all kinds of foods served at the buffet. It includes bacon, eggs, toast, sausage, waffles, pancakes, cereal, and fruit.

Guest That sounds good. [3]What if I want to order from the menu instead?

Waiter You can do that, but you will need to pay extra then. Would you like to order from the a la carte menu?

Guest Hmm . . . No, thank you. I'll try the buffet.

Key Expressions

1 Would you like to have the breakfast buffet or see a menu?   조식 뷔페를 드시겠습니까, 아니면 메뉴를 보시겠습니까?

손님에게 두 가지 선택 사항 중 어떤 것을 원하는지 묻는 표현으로, 동사 like 대신 prefer나 want를 사용할 수도 있다.

Would you prefer orange or apple juice?   오렌지 주스와 사과 주스 중 어느 것을 드시겠습니까?
Which one do you want, a double room or a suite?   더블룸과 스위트룸 중 어떤 것을 원하십니까?

2 Are you a guest at the hotel?   이 호텔의 투숙객이십니까?

상대가 호텔의 투숙객인지 방문객인지 확인할 때 쓰는 말이다.

Are you staying at this hotel?   이 호텔에 묵고 계십니까?

3 What if I want to order from the menu instead?   그 대신 메뉴에서 주문을 하고 싶으면요?

조식 뷔페를 무료로 이용할 수 있는 손님이 메뉴에서 주문을 하고 싶으면 어떻게 해야 하는지 묻는 말이다. What if ~?는 '~하면 어떻게 되나요?'라는 뜻으로, 그 대신 What happens if ~?를 사용할 수도 있다.

What if I forget to make a reservation?   예약하는 것을 잊으면 어떻게 되나요?
What happens if I check out late?   체크아웃을 늦게 하면 어떻게 되나요?

💡 Useful Phrases

You will need to V   ~하셔야 할 것 입니다.

You will need to pay extra then.   그러면 차액을 지불하셔야 할 것입니다.
You will need to make a reservation to use the spa.   스파를 사용하시려면 예약을 하셔야 할 것입니다.
You will need to pay an additional fee.   추가 비용을 지불하셔야 할 것입니다.

Basic Drills

A 주어진 문장에 어울리는 대답을 고르세요.

1 Would you like to have the breakfast buffet or see a menu? •

2 Hotel guests can enjoy a complimentary breakfast buffet. •

3 What if I want to order from the menu instead? •

• **ⓐ** That sounds good.

• **ⓑ** I'm sorry, but I haven't decided yet.

• **ⓒ** You can do that, but you will need to pay extra then.

B 괄호 안의 말을 순서대로 배열하여 주어진 의미를 영어로 표현하세요.

1 조식 뷔페를 드시겠습니까, 아니면 메뉴를 보시겠습니까? (to have / see a menu / the breakfast buffet / or / would you like)

→ ____

2 이 호텔의 투숙객이십니까? (you / the hotel / a guest / at / are)

→ ____

3 그 대신 메뉴에서 주문을 하고 싶으면요? (want to / the menu / what if / order / I / from / instead)

→ ____

Buildup Activities 대화를 듣고 빈칸을 채운 후 주어진 질문에 답하세요.

Waitress	Good morning. Welcome to the Skyview restaurant. Would you prefer to have the breakfast ____________ or to see a menu?
Guest	Good morning. Actually, I haven't made up my mind yet.
Waitress	Are you ____________ here at the hotel?
Guest	Yes, I am. Why?
Waitress	All ____________ receive a complimentary breakfast buffet. The buffet has many kinds of foods. For example, you can get cereal, ____________, bacon, sausages, eggs, yogurt, and fruit.
Guest	Wow, that's a good deal. But what if I decide to ____________ from the menu instead?
Waitress	In that case, you will have to pay money. So do you want to order from the ____________ menu?
Guest	That's all right. I think I'll just have the buffet.

🎧 06-03

1 What food does the waitress NOT mention?

ⓐ waffles　　　　ⓑ fruit　　　　ⓒ pancakes

2 What does the guest decide to do?

ⓐ order from the a la carte menu　　　ⓑ have the breakfast buffet　　　ⓒ go to another restaurant

Conversation II 

다음 대화를 듣고 파트너와 함께 대화를 연습해 보세요.

🎧 06-04

Drinks at the Bar

Bartender Good evening, sir. [1]What can I get you to drink?

Guest Hello. What kind of draft beer do you have?

Bartender [2]We have Vanguard, Daeng, and a couple of local beers on tap.

Guest Hmm . . . Maybe I'll get something else.

Bartender Why don't you have a margarita or a mimosa? Both of them are very popular drinks here.

Guest What's in a mimosa? I'm not familiar with it.

Bartender [3]A mimosa is half orange juice and half champagne. It's simple to make but tastes really good.

Guest Okay. I'd like to have one of those, please.

Key Expressions

1 What can I get you to drink?   마실 것은 무엇으로 드릴까요?

손님에게 무엇을 마실지 묻는 표현이다. to drink를 생략하고 What can I get you?만으로도 상황에 따라 식당에서는 음식을, 바에서는 음료나 주류를 주문받을 수 있다.

What can I get you?   무엇을 드릴까요?
What would you like to drink?   무엇을 마시고 싶으신가요?

2 We have Vanguard, Daeng, and a couple of local beers on tap.
뱅가드, 댕, 그리고 몇 가지 현지 생맥주가 있습니다.

어떤 종류의 맥주가 있는지 설명하는 표현으로, 병맥주인 경우에는 맥주 이름만 말하면 되고, 생맥주인 경우에는 맥주 이름 뒤에 on tap을 덧붙인다.

You can choose from Vanguard, Daeng, and a couple of local beers on tap.
뱅가드, 댕, 그리고 몇 가지 현지 생맥주 중에서 고르실 수 있습니다.

There are many international beers such as Steller Airs, Champ, and Forest.
스텔러 에어즈, 챔프, 그리고 포레스트와 같은 세계적인 맥주가 많이 있습니다.

3 A mimosa is half orange juice and half champagne.   미모사는 오렌지 주스와 샴페인을 반반 섞은 것입니다.

칵테일에 무엇이 들어가는지 설명하는 표현이다.

A shandy is equal parts beer and lemonade.   샌디는 맥주와 레모네이드를 같은 비율로 섞은 것입니다.
A gin and tonic is one shot of gin topped up with tonic water.   진토닉은 한 잔의 진에 토닉 워터를 보충한 것입니다.

💡 Useful Phrases

맛을 나타내는 표현

It tastes really good.
그것은 맛이 정말 좋습니다.

It tastes sweet and sour.
그것은 달고 시큼합니다.

It has a sweet flavor.
그것은 단맛이 납니다.

It is like grape juice with a bit of bitterness.
그것은 약간의 쓴맛이 나는 포도 주스와 같습니다.

Basic Drills

A 주어진 문장에 어울리는 대답을 고르세요.

1 It's simple to make but tastes really good.

2 What kind of draft beer do you have?

3 Why don't you have a margarita or a mimosa?

ⓐ What's in a mimosa?

ⓑ We have Vanguard, Daeng, and a couple of local beers on tap.

ⓒ Okay. I'd like to have one of those, please.

B 괄호 안의 말을 순서대로 배열하여 주어진 의미를 영어로 표현하세요.

1 마실 것은 무엇으로 드릴까요? (I / can / get you / what / to drink)

→ ....

2 뱅가드, 댕, 그리고 몇 가지 현지 생맥주가 있습니다.
(a couple of / Vanguard, Daeng / on tap / and / we have / local beers)

→ ....

3 미모사는 오렌지 주스와 샴페인을 반반 섞은 것입니다. (is / half champagne / a mimosa / half orange juice / and)

→ ....

Buildup Activities 대화를 듣고 빈칸을 채운 후 주어진 질문에 답하세요.

Bartender	Good evening, ma'am. Would you care for ______________ to drink?
Guest	Hi there. What ______________ do you have?
Bartender	We have Vanguard, Daeng, and three local beers on tap.
Guest	Hmm . . . Maybe I'll order something else.
Bartender	How about having a margarita or a mint julep? Both are ______________ drinks with many customers.
Guest	What's in a ______________? I've never had one before.
Bartender	A mint julep contains ______________, sugar cubes, and mint leaves. Making it is simple, and it ______________.
Guest	Okay. I'll try one of those, please.

🎧 06-05

1 What does the guest ask about first?

ⓐ draft beers

ⓑ cocktails

ⓒ bottled beers

2 What does the guest order?

ⓐ a margarita

ⓑ a beer

ⓒ a mint julep

Job Simulation **Ⅰ**

A 〈보기〉에서 적절한 말을 찾아 각 그림의 상황에 맞는 대화를 완성하세요.

1

2

3

B 주어진 세 가지 상황을 이용하여 파트너와 함께 각 상황에 맞는 대화를 연습해 보세요.

Situation	ⓐ	ⓑ
1	staying here	a variety of foods
2	a guest here	many different foods
3	a paying guest at the hotel	a lot of foods

Waiter	Are you ⓐ __________________?
Guest	Yes, I am. Why do you ask?
Waiter	Hotel guests can enjoy a complimentary breakfast buffet. There are ⓑ __________________ served at the buffet. It includes bacon, eggs, toast, sausage, waffles, pancakes, cereal, and fruit.
Guest	That sounds good.

Job Simulation II

A 〈보기〉에서 적절한 말을 찾아 각 그림의 상황에 맞는 대화를 완성하세요.

보기

We have several local beers on tap.

What would you like to have?

It's a combination of vodka and orange juice.

1

What sort of draft beer do you offer?

2

Perhaps I'll get something else to drink.

3

What's in a screwdriver?

B 주어진 세 가지 상황을 이용하여 파트너와 함께 각 상황에 맞는 대화를 연습해 보세요.

Situation	ⓐ	ⓑ	ⓒ
1	bottled beer	both domestic and imported bottled beer	How about having
2	whiskey	blended and single-malt whiskey	What do you think of
3	wine	some local wines	Would you care for

Guest What kind of ⓐ ____________________ do you have?

Bartender We have ⓑ ____________________ .

Guest Hmm . . . Maybe I'll get something else.

Bartender ⓒ ____________________ a margarita or a mimosa? Both of them are very popular drinks here.

다음 지문을 읽고 음성을 들어 보세요.

🎧 06-06

Types of Hotel Breakfasts

Hotels around the world provide different types of breakfasts. The four most common ones are the continental breakfast, the American breakfast, the English breakfast, and the breakfast buffet. A continental breakfast is a light meal. It includes bread, juice, and a hot drink such as coffee or tea. Some hotels also serve fruit, yogurt, and cereal with it. An American breakfast includes two eggs, bacon or sausage, toast, pancakes, cereal, juice, fruit, and coffee or tea. An English breakfast is [1]more substantial than both a continental breakfast and an American breakfast. It usually has sausage, bacon, a grilled tomato, mushrooms, eggs, toast, and tea or coffee. A breakfast buffet typically has all kinds of food. Guests can select cereal, bacon, eggs, sausage, toast, pancakes, and other breakfast foods. There is also usually [2]a large selection of fruit as well as milk, juice, coffee, and tea.

Words & Phrases

common usual; regular   **substantial** large; heavy   **grilled** cooked over a fire   **typically** usually; normally   **selection** a choice; a variety

Basic Grammar

1 형용사의 비교급 + than   ~보다 더 ~한

일반적으로 형용사의 비교급은 형용사 뒤에 –er을 붙여서 나타내지만, 본문의 substantial 같이 음절이 긴 형용사의 경우 형용사 앞에 more를 붙여서 비교급을 만든다. 참고로, 형용사의 비교급 앞에 still, even, much, far, a lot 같은 부사를 넣으면 '훨씬'이라는 강조의 의미를 더할 수 있다.

Buying a one-day transportation pass around the city is cheaper than buying a ticket for each ride.
시내 대중 교통 1일 이용권을 사는 것이 탑승할 때마다 표를 사는 것보다 더 경제적입니다.

2 B as well as A   A뿐만 아니라 B도

B as well A는 'A뿐만 아니라 B도'라는 뜻으로서 문법적으로 대등한 특징을 가진 것을 나열할 때 사용한다. 같은 의미로 not only A but (also) B를 사용할 수도 있다.

You can have not only coffee but also orange juice.   커피뿐만 아니라 오렌지 주스도 드실 수 있습니다.

TIPS & TIPS

못 드시는 음식이 있다면 미리 말씀해 주세요.

이런저런 이유로 특정 음식을 먹지 못하는 사람들이 있습니다. 알레르기가 있는 사람도 있고, 종교적이거나 개인적인 이유로 먹지 않는 사람도 있습니다. 이유야 어찌 되었던 호텔에서는 이런 사람들을 위해 레스토랑이나 룸서비스 메뉴에 들어가는 재료를 상세하게 알립니다. 재료를 미리 공개함으로써 손님들에게 자신이 못 먹는 음식을 피할 수 있도록 배려하는 것입니다. 더 나아가 호텔들은 손님들에게 자신이 먹지 않는 음식이나 재료를 미리 호텔에 알릴 것을 권장합니다. 그러면 호텔이 각각의 손님에게 어떤 메뉴는 먹어도 되고, 어떤 것은 안 되는지 더 자세히 알려 줄 수 있기 때문입니다.

Hotel Facilities

UNIT 07

다음은 호텔을 이용하는 고객들의 이야기입니다. 각 고객이 이용하고자 하는 호텔 시설을 사진에서 고르세요.

1 "I have to print something. I am attending a seminar tomorrow."

2 "I want to buy a leather wallet for my son as a graduation gift."

3 "I need to lift weights because I like to stay in good shape."

4 "I'd like to cool off and have fun with my children."

ⓐ fitness center

ⓑ indoor pool

ⓒ business center

ⓓ duty-free shop

Vocabulary 주어진 단어와 어울리는 의미를 고르세요.

1 staple •   • ⓐ to set up; to organize

2 be familiar with •   • ⓑ a place where people change clothes

3 take care of •   • ⓒ to do something

4 arrange •   • ⓓ to know about; to know how to use

5 dressing room •   • ⓔ to join papers together with a small piece of metal

Warmup Listening 문장을 듣고 그에 맞는 대답을 고르세요.

1 ⓐ I'd like a single room, please.   ⓑ I'm in room 430.

2 ⓐ The dressing room is over there.   ⓑ Why don't you get dressed now?

3 ⓐ The letter has been translated.   ⓑ Sure. I can find one.

🎧 07-01

Conversation Ⅰ

다음 대화를 듣고 파트너와 함께 대화를 연습해 보세요.

🎧 07-02

At the Fitness Center

Fitness Center Attendant Welcome to the Royal Hotel's fitness center. [1]What is your room number?

Guest I'm staying in room 906. My name is Aaron Summers.

Fitness Center Attendant Thank you, Mr. Summers. Do you have any questions about the equipment here?

Guest No, I don't. I'm familiar with everything. But where can I change into my workout clothes?

Fitness Center Attendant [2]The men's dressing room is over there to the right.

Guest Thank you. Can I take a shower in there, too?

Fitness Center Attendant Yes, you can. You may also want to use our sauna. [3]To get to it, go through that door on the left.

Guest You've been very helpful. Thank you so much.

Key Expressions

1 **What is your room number?** 객실 번호가 어떻게 되십니까?

호텔의 시설을 이용하려는 손님에게 손님이 묵고 있는 객실 번호를 묻는 말로, Can [Could] you tell me ~?를 이용하면 좀 더 정중한 표현이 된다.

Can [Could] you tell me what your room number is? 객실 번호가 몇 번인지 말씀해 주시겠습니까?

2 **The men's dressing room is over there to the right.** 남자 탈의실은 저기 오른쪽에 있습니다.

탈의실의 위치를 안내할 때 사용할 수 있는 문장으로, changing room이나 locker room으로도 '탈의실'을 의미할 수 있다.

The locker room is located right next to the bathroom. 탈의실은 화장실 바로 옆에 있습니다.
You will find the changing room on your left. 손님의 왼쪽에서 탈의실을 찾으실 수 있을 겁니다.

3 **To get to it, go through that door on the left.** 그곳에 가려면 저 왼쪽 문을 통과하세요.

호텔 시설의 위치를 설명할 때 사용할 수 있는 문장이다.

Follow the arrows to the gym. 화살표를 따라 헬스장으로 가세요.
Take the second door on your right. You will find the ballroom there. 오른쪽의 두 번째 문으로 들어가세요. 연회장을 찾으실 수 있을 겁니다.

 **Useful Phrases**

이용 가능한 시설을 안내하는 표현

You may want to use our sauna. 저희 (호텔) 사우나를 이용해 보세요.
Feel free to use our pool. 저희 (호텔) 수영장을 마음껏 이용하세요.
There is the business center that you can use. 손님께서 이용하실 수 있는 비즈니스 센터가 있습니다.

Basic Drills

A 주어진 문장에 어울리는 대답을 고르세요.

1 What is your room number?   •   • ⓐ I'm staying in room 906.

2 Where can I change into my workout clothes?   •   • ⓑ The men's dressing room is over there to the right.

3 Do you have any questions about the equipment here?   •   • ⓒ No, I don't. I'm familiar with everything.

B 괄호 안의 말을 순서대로 배열하여 주어진 의미를 영어로 표현하세요.

1 객실 번호가 어떻게 되십니까? (number / your / is / room / what)

→ ____

2 남자 탈의실은 저기 오른쪽에 있습니다. (over there / is / the men's dressing room / to the right)

→ ____

3 그곳에 가려면 저 왼쪽 문을 통과하세요. (go through / on the left / get to it / to / that door)

→ ____

Buildup Activities   대화를 듣고 빈칸을 채운 후 주어진 질문에 답하세요.

Fitness Center Attendant	Welcome to the ______________ at the Royal Hotel. Could you tell me your room number, please?
Guest	Sure. I'm in room 303. I'm Kelly Hopkins.
Fitness Center Attendant	Thank you, Ms. Hopkins. Do you need me to tell you how to use any of the ______________ here?
Guest	No, I don't. I work out at a gym regularly. But can you tell me where the ______________ is?
Fitness Center Attendant	Of course. The dressing room is on the ______________ of the room.
Guest	Thank you. Can I ______________ there as well?
Fitness Center Attendant	Yes, you can. We also have a sauna. It's located behind the ______________.
Guest	Thanks a lot for your assistance.

🎧 07-03

1 **What does the guest tell the fitness center attendant?**
ⓐ She needs help with the machines.
ⓑ She has visited the hotel's fitness center before.
ⓒ She often exercises at a health club.

2 **Where is the dressing room?**
ⓐ behind the cycling machines   ⓑ on the other side of the room   ⓒ next to the entrance

Conversation II

다음 대화를 듣고 파트너와 함께 대화를 연습해 보세요.

🎧 07-04

At the Business Center

Guest	Hello. My name is Harold Carter. I called a few minutes ago about using the scanner.
Business Center Attendant	Yes, Mr. Carter. ¹You spoke with me. The scanner is right here. ²Do you know how to use it?
Guest	Yes, I know how to scan documents.
Business Center Attendant	Great. Is there anything else you need?
Guest	Yes, there is. Can you please copy these papers? I need 10 black-and-white copies, and they should be stapled together.
Business Center Attendant	I'll get right on it.
Guest	There's one more thing. I need a Chinese translator for a meeting tomorrow morning. ³Can you arrange one for me?
Business Center Attendant	Sure, I can do that. I'll take care of that after I make your copies.

Key Expressions

1 You spoke with me. 저와 통화하셨습니다.

조금 전에 전화로 문의를 했다는 손님에게 자신이 전화를 받았다고 응대할 때 쓸 수 있는 표현이다.

I was the one on the phone with you.   제가 손님과 통화했던 사람입니다.
Of course, I remember you.   네, 기억납니다.

2 Do you know how to use it? 이것을 사용하는 법을 알고 계십니까?

호텔 기물의 사용법을 알고 있는지 손님에게 묻는 말이다. how to V를 이용하여 '~하는 법'이라는 의미를 표현할 수 있다.

Can you tell me how to make a copy?   복사하는 법을 알려 주시겠어요?
Let me show you how to use this.   이것을 사용하는 법을 알려 드리겠습니다.

3 Can you arrange one for me? (통역사) 한 명을 준비해 주시겠어요?

손님이 호텔 측에 무엇을 요청할 때 동사 arrange(준비하다)를 사용할 수 있다. 그 외에 get(마련하다, 구하다)이나 find(찾다) 등을 이용할 수도 있다.

Would you get me a suite?   스위트룸을 하나 마련해 주시겠어요?
Could you find me a meeting room in the hotel?   호텔 내의 회의실을 하나 찾아 주시겠어요?

💡 Useful Phrases

Is there anything else you need? 더 필요한 것 있으십니까?

= Would you like anything else?   = Can I help you with anything else?   = Do you have everything you need?

Basic Drills

A 주어진 문장에 어울리는 대답을 고르세요.

1 Can you arrange one for me?　　　　•　　　•　ⓐ Sure, I can do that.

2 Is there anything else you need?　　•　　　•　ⓑ Yes, there is. Can you please copy these papers?

3 Do you know how to use it?　　　　•　　　•　ⓒ Yes, I know how to scan documents.

B 괄호 안의 말을 순서대로 배열하여 주어진 의미를 영어로 표현하세요.

1 저와 통화하셨습니다. (me / spoke / you / with)

　⇒ ....

2 이것을 사용하는 법을 알고 계십니까? (know / do / use it / you / how to)

　⇒ ....

3 (통역사) 한 명을 준비해 주시겠어요? (for me / you / one / arrange / can)

　⇒ ....

Buildup Activities　대화를 듣고 빈칸을 채운 후 주어진 질문에 답하세요.

Guest	Good afternoon. I'm Jessica Stewart. I called .... about using the scanner.
Business Center Attendant	Yes, Ms. Stewart. You talked to me. The .... is over there. Do you require any assistance with it?
Guest	That's all right. I know how to ....
Business Center Attendant	Excellent. Can I do anything else for you?
Guest	Yes, please. Would you make 20 copies of this report for me? I need 3 ....
Business Center Attendant	Of course. I'll start doing that right now.
Guest	I need something else, too. I require a Russian .... for a meeting tomorrow at one. Can you find one for me?
Business Center Attendant	That will be no problem at all. Let me make the copies first. Then, I will make the necessary .... for a translator.

🎧 07-05

1 What does the business center attendant ask the guest?

　ⓐ if she can use the scanner

　ⓑ if she can speak Russian

　ⓒ if she needs to send a letter

2 What does the guest NOT need to do?

　ⓐ make some color copies　　　　ⓑ get a translator　　　　ⓒ receive a telephone call

A 〈보기〉에서 적절한 말을 찾아 각 그림의 상황에 맞는 대화를 완성하세요.

보기

What room are you staying in?	How can I get to the sauna?	Where can I put on my gym clothes?

1

I'm on the top floor in room 1020.

2

The dressing room is right over there by the wall.

3

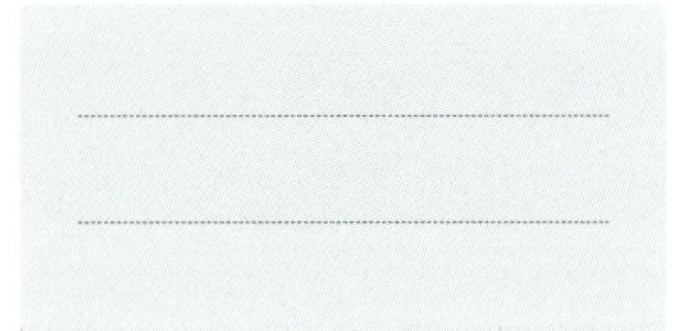

To get to it, just go through that door over there.

B 주어진 세 가지 상황을 이용하여 파트너와 함께 각 상황에 맞는 대화를 연습해 보세요.

Situation	ⓐ	ⓑ	ⓒ
1	get dressed	changing room	use the indoor swimming pool
2	change clothes	locker room	sit in the Jacuzzi
3	put on my shorts and T-shirt	dressing room	visit the massage room

Guest	Where can I ⓐ __________ ?
Fitness Center Attendant	The ⓑ __________ is over there to the right.
Guest	Thank you. Can I take a shower in there, too?
Fitness Center Attendant	Yes, you can. You may also ⓒ __________ . To get to it, go through that door on the left.

A 〈보기〉에서 적절한 말을 찾아 각 그림의 상황에 맞는 대화를 완성하세요.

보 기

| Is there anything else I can do for you? | I called the business center a while ago. | Yes, I'll do that in just a couple of minutes. |

1

Yes, you talked to me on the phone.

2

Yes, please. Can you mail this letter for me?

3

Can you arrange a translator for me?

B 주어진 세 가지 상황을 이용하여 파트너와 함께 각 상황에 맞는 대화를 연습해 보세요.

Situation	ⓐ	ⓑ
1	color copies	a secretary
2	full-sized copies	an interpreter
3	copies of the front and back pages	a lawyer

Guest	Can you please copy these papers? I need 10 ⓐ _______.
Business Center Attendant	I'll get right on it.
Guest	There's one more thing. I need ⓑ _______ for a meeting tomorrow morning.
Business Center Attendant	I'll take care of that after making the copies.

다음 지문을 읽고 음성을 들어 보세요.

🎧 07-06

Types of Shops inside Hotels

Modern hotels, especially big ones, have more than just rooms for guests. They also have many different kinds of shops. The [1]most common shops in hotels are restaurants. Most hotels have at least one, and larger hotels may have several restaurants. Each of these restaurants has a different theme, and one is usually a buffet restaurant. Bars are commonplace in hotels as well. Some hotels may also have nightclubs or casinos in their basements. Hotels usually have gift shops. So guests can buy souvenirs in them. They have small convenience stores for buying drinks and snacks, too. There is often a place for guests [2]to exchange currency as well as a tailor shop for people to buy custom-made clothes. Some of the largest hotels even have large numbers of duty-free shops. These shops sell all kinds of clothes, alcohol, jewelry, and watches. When there are so many shops in a hotel, guests do not have to go outside to do their shopping.

Words & Phrases

theme a concept; a subject   **commonplace** normal; usual   **casino** a place where people can gamble   **souvenir** a reminder of a trip; a keepsake   **currency** money

Basic Grammar

1 most + 형용사 [부사]   가장 ~한 [가장 ~하게]

most는 본문의 common 같이 음절이 2개 이상인 형용사 또는 부사를 최상급으로 만들 때 사용되며, '가장'이라는 의미를 나타낸다. 참고로 most hotels처럼 'most + 명사'로 쓰이는 경우, most는 '대부분의'라는 의미를 나타내는 형용사이다.

This suite has the most beautiful view over the beach.　이 스위트룸은 해변이 내려다보이는 가장 아름다운 전망을 보여 줍니다.
Our most popular dish in this restaurant is Atlantic salmon.　이 레스토랑에서 가장 인기 있는 요리는 대서양 연어 요리입니다.

2 to부정사의 형용사적 용법

to부정사가 명사를 뒤에서 수식할 때는 '~하는', '~할'이라는 형용사의 의미로 쓰인다. to부정사 바로 앞에 'for + 목적격'이 오면 to부정사의 행위의 주체도 알 수 있다. 즉 a place for guests to exchange currency는 '손님들이(for guests) 화폐를 교환하는(to exchange currency) 장소(a place)'라는 뜻이다.

Here are three elevators only for guests to use.　여기 고객 전용 엘리베이터 세 대가 있습니다.
I have a form for you to fill out.　손님께서 작성하실 양식이 있습니다.

TIPS & TIPS

객실에는 무엇이 있을까요?

호텔에는 모든 객실마다 침대, 의자, 욕조나 샤워 부스가 딸린 욕실이 있습니다. 이에 더해, 대부분의 경우, TV, 전화기, 소형 냉장고도 비치되어 있습니다. 소형 냉장고에는 보통 생수가 들어 있고, 과자나 음료가 채워져 있는 미니바도 있습니다. 커피 메이커나 공기 청정기가 있는 경우도 있으며, 에어컨이나 난방기, 그리고 이것들을 조작할 수 있는 리모컨도 보통 비치되어 있습니다. 객실에 고객이 귀중품을 넣을 수 있는 소형 금고가 있는 호텔도 있고, 객실 내에서 무선 인터넷을 이용할 수 있는 호텔도 많습니다. 욕실에는 보통 비누, 샴푸, 로션, 목욕용 가운, 그리고 슬리퍼가 있습니다.

Room Service

Warmup

다음은 호텔 객실에 비치되어 있는 비품들입니다. 각 비품의 이름을 아래에서 찾아 써 보세요.

1

2

3

4

in-room safe	bathrobe	minibar	air conditioner

Vocabulary 주어진 단어와 어울리는 의미를 고르세요.

1 honeymoon •

2 cost •

3 total •

4 thoughtful •

5 charge •

• ⓐ to require a certain amount of money to pay for something

• ⓑ a trip that newlyweds take after getting married

• ⓒ kind; considerate

• ⓓ a complete price; a full price

• ⓔ to bill

Warmup Listening 문장을 듣고 그에 맞는 대답을 고르세요.

1 ⓐ The steak sounds nice.　　ⓑ I ordered pork chops.

2 ⓐ Yes, I'm going to do that.　　ⓑ Yes, I already charged it.

3 ⓐ Yes, the bags are on the floor.　　ⓑ That would be great. Thanks.

🎧 08-01

Conversation I

다음 대화를 듣고 파트너와 함께 대화를 연습해 보세요.

🎧 08-02

Taking Room Service Orders on the Phone

Guest	Hello. This is Amy Carter in room 943. I want to get some room service, please.
Telephone Operator	Of course. [1]What would you like to order?
Guest	I want to have the roasted chicken dinner, please. I'd like some French fries, too.
Telephone Operator	No problem, ma'am. How about something to drink?
Guest	That's a good idea. I'll take two bottles of cola.
Telephone Operator	No problem. [2]Will you be charging this to your room?
Guest	Yes, I will. How much is the total?
Telephone Operator	It costs $30.95. [3]Someone will deliver the food to your room in about twenty minutes.

Key Expressions

1 What would you like to order?   무엇을 주문하시겠습니까?

룸서비스로 어떤 음식이나 음료를 주문하겠는지 손님에게 묻는 말이다. 동사 order(주문하다) 대신 get이니 have를 쓸 수도 있디.

What can I get you?   무엇을 드릴까요?
Have you decided what to order?   무엇을 주문하실지 결정하셨습니까?

2 Will you be charging this to your room?   이것을 객실 요금으로 청구하시겠습니까?

호텔에 묵으면서 어떤 서비스를 이용한 손님에게 서비스 이용료를 객실 앞으로 달아놓을지 묻는 말이다.

Would you like to put it on your tab?   이것을 손님의 계산서에 넣으시겠습니까?
Do you want me to put this on your account?   이것을 손님의 계산서에 넣어 드릴까요?

3 Someone will deliver the food to your room in about twenty minutes.

누군가가 약 20분 후에 손님 객실로 음식을 배달해 드릴 것입니다.

룸서비스로 주문한 음식이 언제 배달되는지 설명하는 문장이다. 전치사 in은 시간의 경과를 나타내며 '~ 후에'라는 뜻으로 사용된다.

Your order will be ready in 35 to 40 minutes.   손님께서 주문하신 것은 35분에서 40분 후에 준비될 것입니다.
It will take about 30 minutes to bring the food up to your room.   음식을 손님 객실로 가져다 드리는데 30분 정도 걸릴 것입니다.

💡 Useful Phrases

How about something to drink?   음료는 어떻게 하시겠습니까?

= What about something to drink?   = Would you like something to drink?   = Would you care for a drink?

Basic Drills

A 주어진 문장에 어울리는 대답을 고르세요.

1 Will you be charging this to your room? •

2 I want to get some room service, please. •

3 How about something to drink? •

• **ⓐ** What would you like to order?

• **ⓑ** Yes, I will. How much is the total?

• **ⓒ** I'll take two bottles of cola.

B 괄호 안의 말을 순서대로 배열하여 주어진 의미를 영어로 표현하세요.

1 무엇을 주문하시겠습니까? (you / like to / would / order / what)

→

2 이것을 객실 요금으로 청구하시겠습니까? (be charging / your room / will you / this / to)

→

3 누군가가 약 20분 후에 손님 객실로 음식을 배달해 드릴 것입니다.
(the food / about twenty minutes / to your room / will deliver / someone / in)

→

Buildup Activities 대화를 듣고 빈칸을 채운 후 주어진 질문에 답하세요.

Guest	Hello. I'm Paul Stewart in room 357. May I please order some ________ ?
Telephone Operator	Yes, you may. What would you like to have, sir?
Guest	I'll take the sirloin steak dinner. I'd also like a ________ with it.
Telephone Operator	All right. Would you care for something to ________ ?
Guest	Yes, please. I want some ________, please.
Telephone Operator	No problem. How will you be paying for your meal?
Guest	I'll pay ________. What's the total?
Telephone Operator	Your meal costs $35. Your food will ________ within fifteen minutes.

⌂ 08-03

1 What does the guest NOT order?
- **ⓐ** a cola
- **ⓑ** a steak
- **ⓒ** a baked potato

2 How will the guest pay for the meal?
- **ⓐ** by charging it to the room
- **ⓑ** by using cash
- **ⓒ** by using a credit card

Conversation **II**

다음 대화를 듣고 파트너와 함께 대화를 연습해 보세요.

🎧 08-04

Making Special Deliveries

Room Service Clerk	Good afternoon. Room service, sir.
Guest	[1]I'm sorry, but there must be some mistake. I didn't order anything.
Room Service Clerk	You reserved a room here for your honeymoon, right?
Guest	That's correct.
Room Service Clerk	[2]The Royal Hotel provides guests on their honeymoon with a complimentary bottle of champagne and a box of chocolates.
Guest	What a pleasant surprise. That's very thoughtful.
Room Service Clerk	[3]Shall I put them here on the table? I brought some ice and glasses for you as well.
Guest	Yes, that would be great. Thank you.

Key Expressions

1 I'm sorry, but there must be some mistake.   죄송하지만, 무슨 착오가 있는 것 같아요.

무엇인가 잘못되었다는 표현으로, 강한 추측을 나타내는 조동사 must가 사용되었다.

I am afraid that you have the wrong room.   죄송하지만, 방을 잘못 찾으신 것 같아요.
This cannot be meant for us.   이것은 저희 것일 리가 없어요.

2 The Royal Hotel provides guests on their honeymoon with a complimentary bottle of champagne and a box of chocolates.

로얄 호텔은 신혼 여행 중이신 손님들께 샴페인 한 병과 초콜릿 한 상자를 무료로 제공합니다.

호텔에서 신혼 부부에게 소정의 선물을 제공한다고 안내하는 표현이다. 형용사 complimentary는 '무료의'라는 뜻이다. 그 밖에도 free (of charge)나 on the house 등을 써서 어떤 것이 무료임을 나타낼 수 있다.

These are free of charge.   이것들은 무료입니다.
These roses are from the Royal Hotel. Of course, they are on the house.   이 장미꽃은 로얄 호텔에서 드리는 것입니다. 물론 무료입니다.

3 Shall I put them here on the table?   여기 테이블 위에 놓을까요?

룸서비스로 가져온 것을 어디에 놓을지 묻는 표현이다. 의문문에서 상대의 의향을 물을 때 조동사 shall을 사용할 수 있다.

Shall I put your bags by the couch?   소파 옆에 가방을 놓을까요?
Where do you want me to put these?   이것들을 어디에 놓을까요?

💡 Useful Phrases

That's very thoughtful. 정말 친절하시네요.

= That is very kind of you.　　= What a wonderful gesture.
= How lovely!　　　　　　　　= I am very touched.

Basic Drills

A 주어진 문장에 어울리는 대답을 고르세요.

1 Good afternoon. Room service.   •   • **ⓐ** That's correct.

2 You reserved a room here for your honeymoon, right?   •   • **ⓑ** Yes, that would be great.

3 Shall I put them here on the table?   •   • **ⓒ** I'm sorry, but there must be some mistake.

B 괄호 안의 말을 순서대로 배열하여 주어진 의미를 영어로 표현하세요.

1 죄송하지만, 무슨 착오가 있는 것 같아요. (I'm sorry / there / but / some mistake / must be)

→ ____

2 로얄 호텔은 신혼 여행 중이신 손님들께 샴페인 한 병과 초콜릿 한 상자를 무료로 제공합니다.
(on their honeymoon / and a box of chocolates / guests / with a complimentary bottle of champagne / the Royal Hotel / provides)

→ ____

3 여기 테이블 위에 놓을까요? (the table / shall I / here / on / put them)

→ ____

Buildup Activities   대화를 듣고 빈칸을 채운 후 주어진 질문에 답하세요.

Room Service Clerk	Good evening. _______________ .
Guest	I'm sorry, but you must be _______________ . I never called room service to order anything.
Room Service Clerk	That's right. But you're here on your _______________ , aren't you?
Guest	That's right.
Room Service Clerk	The Royal Hotel provides honeymooners with a complimentary bottle of champagne as well as _______________ .
Guest	Thank you so much. That's a nice _______________ .
Room Service Clerk	Should I put these on the table here? I've got some ice and _______________ as well.
Guest	That's perfect. Thanks a lot. My husband and I really appreciate it.

🎧 08-05

1 Why is the guest staying at the hotel?
- **ⓐ** She just got married.
- **ⓑ** She is on business.
- **ⓒ** She is on a family trip.

2 What does the room service clerk bring the guest?
- **ⓐ** food and beverages
- **ⓑ** roses and champagne
- **ⓒ** chocolate and wine

Job Simulation Ⅰ

A 〈보기〉에서 적절한 말을 찾아 각 그림의 상황에 맞는 대화를 완성하세요.

보 기

Someone will visit your room twenty minutes from now.	No, I'll pay for it with my credit card.	What food would you like to order?

1

I'd like the seafood pasta dinner, please.

2

Are you going to charge this to your room?

3

When will my meal arrive?

B 주어진 세 가지 상황을 이용하여 파트너와 함께 각 상황에 맞는 대화를 연습해 보세요.

Situation	ⓐ	ⓑ	ⓒ
1	a double cheeseburger	a cup of coffee	paying cash
2	stir-fried noodles	a glass of white wine	using your credit card
3	a Caesar salad	some orange juice	putting this on your room bill

Telephone Operator	What would you like to order?
Guest	I want to have ⓐ _____________, please. I'd like some French fries, too.
Telephone Operator	No problem, ma'am. How about something to drink?
Guest	That's a good idea. I'll take ⓑ _____________.
Telephone Operator	No problem. Will you be ⓒ _____________?

Job Simulation II

A 〈보기〉에서 적절한 말을 찾아 각 그림의 상황에 맞는 대화를 완성하세요.

I'm sorry, but I think you made a mistake.

Shall I put your items on this table?

The Royal Hotel gives honeymooners complimentary champagne and chocolate.

1

2

3

B 주어진 세 가지 상황을 이용하여 파트너와 함께 각 상황에 맞는 대화를 연습해 보세요.

Situation	ⓐ	ⓑ
1	I believe you made a mistake	a two-layer cake
2	I think there's a problem	a special gift set
3	you must have come here by mistake	some gourmet chocolates

Room Service Clerk	Good afternoon. Room service, sir.
Guest	I'm sorry, but ⓐ _______________. I didn't order anything.
Room Service Clerk	The Royal Hotel provides guests on their honeymoon with a complimentary bottle of champagne and ⓑ _______________.

다음 지문을 읽고 음성을 들어 보세요.

🎧 08-06

Room Service at Hotels

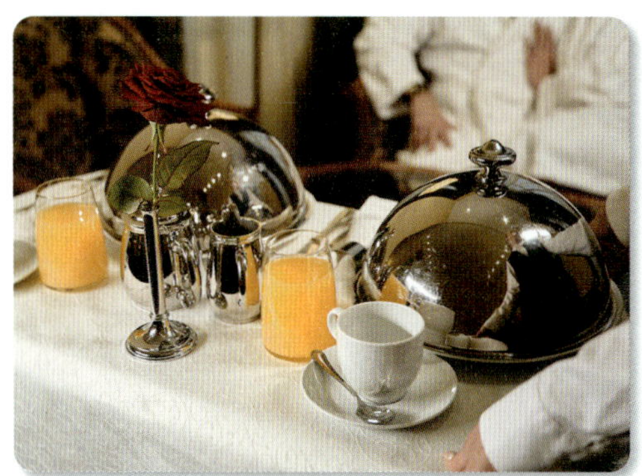

Most medium-sized, large, and luxury hotels provide room service. Room service lets guests order various foods and beverages from a menu. Then, the items they order are brought to their rooms. This allows guests to eat and drink in their own rooms. Room service is typically more expensive than hotel restaurants. However, it provides several advantages. First, guests [1]do not have to leave their rooms, so they can enjoy their meals in privacy. This is especially important for celebrities. Room service is also more convenient for people who are working or meeting clients. And it is normally available 24 hours a day, so guests can order items whenever they like. When the ordered food arrives, it is brought in on a tray. The employee sets up the food and then leaves. The guest can pay for the items at that time or [2]have the order charged to the hotel bill.

Words & Phrases

beverage a drink   **advantage** a benefit   **privacy** the condition of being apart or hidden from others   **celebrity** a famous person
normally usually

Basic Grammar

1 do not have to ～할 필요가 없다

조동사 have to는 '～해야 한다'는 뜻으로, 조동사 must처럼 의무나 필요를 나타낼 때 사용된다. must의 부정형 must not이 '～해서는 안 된다'는 금지의 의미를 나타내는 반면에 have to의 부정형 do not [don't] have to는 '～할 필요가 없다'는 불필요의 의미를 나타낸다.

You don't have to book a seat in advance.   좌석을 미리 예약하실 필요가 없습니다.
You must not smoke in your room.   손님의 객실에서 흡연을 하시면 안 됩니다.

2 have + 목적어 + p.p. (목적어가) ～되도록 하다

5형식 사역동사 have를 사용하여 '(누군가를 시켜) 목적어가 ～되도록 하다'라는 의미를 나타낸다. 과거분사(p.p.)는 수동의 의미이다.

I have my room cleaned every morning.   나는 (누군가를 시켜) 매일 아침 내 방이 청소되도록 한다.
I had my watch fixed.   나는 (누군가를 시켜) 내 시계가 수리되도록 했다.

방 안의 작은 바, 미니바

일부 호텔은 객실에 미니바를 비치해 손님에게 더욱더 편리한 서비스를 제공하고자 합니다. 이는 야심한 시각에 뜬금없이 배가 출출하다든가, 사업상 여행으로 긴 하루를 보내고 돌아와 조용히 술 한잔 하고 싶은 손님에게는 더할 나위 없는 서비스입니다. 미니바는 냉장고나 캐비닛 형태로 제공되는데, 초콜릿, 초콜릿 바, 감자칩 같은 스낵류와, 생수, 콜라, 맥주, 독주같은 마실 것으로 채워져 있습니다. 객실을 한 발짝도 벗어나고 싶지 않을 때는 분명 편할지 모르겠지만, 공짜는 아니라는 사실! 오히려 서비스 이용료와 부가세가 포함되어 시중 가격보다 훨씬 비싼 경우가 많으니 주의하세요. 최근 일부 호텔들은 객실에서 미니바를 없애고 대신 호텔 로비에 편의점을 두기도 합니다. 이리하여 손님은 호텔 밖으로 나가는 번거로움 없이 스낵이나 술을 사 와서 객실 냉장고에 넣어둘 수 있게 되었죠.

Housekeeping Service

Warmup

다음은 객실관리부(Housekeeping Dept.)에서 담당하는 서비스입니다. 각 사진에 해당하는 서비스를 아래에서 찾아 써 보세요.

1 __________

2 __________

3 __________

| babysitting | bed making | laundry |

Vocabulary

주어진 단어와 어울리는 의미를 고르세요.

1 maintenance man •
2 require •
3 be of service •
4 properly •
5 bar •

ⓐ to help someone
ⓑ correctly
ⓒ to need
ⓓ a person who repairs broken equipment
ⓔ a small piece of something, such as soap

Warmup Listening

문장을 듣고 그에 맞는 대답을 고르세요.

1 ⓐ Could I have some more towels, please?　ⓑ This hotel provides many services.

2 ⓐ Yes, I have a problem.　ⓑ The TV won't turn on.

3 ⓐ No, you're not wrong at all.　ⓑ I can't get the air conditioner to work.

🎧 09-01

Conversation Ⅰ

다음 대화를 듣고 파트너와 함께 대화를 연습해 보세요.

🎧 09-02

Providing Housekeeping Services

Housekeeping Order Taker	Good evening. [1]This is Housekeeping. How may I be of service?
Guest	Hello. I'm calling from room 201. Is it possible to get some pillows for my room?
Housekeeping Order Taker	Aren't there already some in your room?
Guest	Yes, there are, but we need two more.
Housekeeping Order Taker	I understand. [2]I'll bring them up to you in a few minutes. Is there anything else you require?
Guest	Yes, there's one more thing. I can't find any soap in the bathroom.
Housekeeping Order Taker	[3]I apologize for the mistake. I shall bring you several small bars of soap.
Guest	Thank you for your assistance.

Key Expressions

1 This is Housekeeping.　객실관리부입니다.

This is ~는 '저는 ~입니다'라는 뜻으로, This is 뒤에 소속 부서나 이름을 넣어 전화 응대 시 사용한다. 이 표현은 전화를 받을 때뿐만 아니라 청소나 관리를 위해 객실에 들어갈 때도 사용할 수 있다.

This is the Housekeeping Department.　객실관리부입니다.
Housekeeping.　객실관리부입니다.

2 I'll bring them up to you in a few minutes.　그것들을 곧 가져다 드리겠습니다.

손님이 요청한 물품을 객실로 가져다 드리겠다는 표현으로, 동사 bring 대신에 deliver(배달하다)나, send(보내다)를 사용할 수도 있다.

I will have someone deliver the items to you soon.　누군가를 시켜 손님께 곧 물품을 배달하도록 하겠습니다.
I will send some pillows up to your room right away.　베개를 즉시 객실로 보내 드리겠습니다.

3 I apologize for the mistake.　실수에 대해 사과 드립니다.

실수에 대해 사과하는 표현으로, for 뒤에는 사과의 이유를 넣을 수 있다.

We apologize for any inconvenience caused.　발생된 불편에 대해 사과 드립니다.
I am really sorry for the trouble.　불편을 끼쳐 대단히 죄송합니다.

💡 Useful Phrases

물건의 단위를 나타내는 표현

a bar of soap　비누 한 개	a box of tissues　화장지 한 갑	a few cotton swabs　면봉 몇 개
a pair of slippers　슬리퍼 한 켤레	a couple of towels　수건 두어 장	a pad of writing paper　메모지 한 묶음
a roll of toilet paper　두루마리 휴지 한 개	a bottle of water　물 한 병	

Basic Drills

A 주어진 문장에 어울리는 대답을 고르세요.

1 I can't find any soap in the bathroom. •

2 Do you require anything else? •

3 Is it possible to get some pillows for my room? •

• **ⓐ** I'll bring them up to you in a few minutes.

• **ⓑ** There's one more thing.

• **ⓒ** I apologize for the mistake.

B 괄호 안의 말을 순서대로 배열하여 주어진 의미를 영어로 표현하세요.

1 객실관리부입니다. (this / Housekeeping / is)

➡ ....

2 그것들을 곧 가져다 드리겠습니다. (to you / I'll / a few minutes / in / bring them up)

➡ ....

3 실수에 대해 사과 드립니다. (I / for / the mistake / apologize)

➡ ....

Buildup Activities 대화를 듣고 빈칸을 채운 후 주어진 질문에 답하세요.

Housekeeping Order Taker	Good afternoon. Housekeeping. What can I do for you?
Guest	Hello. I'm calling from room 409. Can someone bring some .... to my room?
Housekeeping Order Taker	Didn't the .... already leave some on the bed in your room?
Guest	Yes, she did, but I need .... more, please.
Housekeeping Order Taker	I see. Someone .... them in a couple of minutes. Can I do anything else for you?
Guest	Yes, you can. There's no .... in the bathroom.
Housekeeping Order Taker	I'm .... about that. I'll bring a couple of bottles along with your towels.
Guest	Thanks a lot. I appreciate it.

🎧 09-03

1 How many pillows does the guest request?
- **ⓐ** two
- **ⓑ** three
- **ⓒ** four

2 What else does the guest request?
- **ⓐ** a menu
- **ⓑ** some shampoo
- **ⓒ** some soap

다음 대화를 듣고 파트너와 함께 대화를 연습해 보세요.

🎧 09-04

Handling Complaints about Room Problems

Guest	Hi. Is this the Housekeeping Department?
Housekeeping Order Taker	Yes, it is. Is there something I can assist you with?
Guest	I sure hope so. I'm staying in room 824, but there are a couple of problems.
Housekeeping Order Taker	[1]Can you explain what's the matter?
Guest	Sure. First, [2]the shower isn't working properly. I wanted to take a shower, but there's no hot water.
Housekeeping Order Taker	All right. What's the other problem?
Guest	There's something wrong with the Wi-Fi. I can't connect my laptop to the Internet. It's really annoying.
Housekeeping Order Taker	I'm very sorry about that. [3]I'll send a maintenance man to your room right away, ma'am. He should be there within five minutes.

Key Expressions

1 Can you explain what's the matter?　무엇이 문제인지 설명해 주시겠습니까?

문제가 있다는 손님에게 무엇이 문제인지 더 구체적으로 알려 달라고 요청하는 말이다.

Can you tell me in detail?　자세하게 말씀해 주시겠습니까?
Would you tell me what exactly the problems are?　문제가 정확히 무엇인지 말씀해 주시겠습니까?

2 The shower isn't working properly.　샤워기가 제대로 작동하지 않아요.

샤워기가 작동하지 않는다는 표현으로, not working properly는 '제대로 작동하지 않는'이라는 의미로 쓰였다. '고장 난', '작동하지 않는'이라는 의미는 broken이나 out of order 등으로도 나타낼 수 있다.

The electronic kettle seems to be broken.　전기 주전자가 고장 난 것 같아요.
The toilet is out of order.　변기가 고장 났어요.

3 I'll send a maintenance man to your room right away.　수리공을 즉시 객실로 보내 드리겠습니다.

객실로 수리공을 보내서 고장 난 물건이나 시설을 바로 수리해 주겠다는 표현이다.

I will get it fixed immediately.　그것을 즉시 수리해 드리겠습니다.
Someone will be there to fix your TV in no time.　TV를 고쳐 드리러 곧 누군가가 그곳으로 갈 것입니다.

💡 Useful Phrases

right away　즉시, 곧

= immediately	= shortly	= as soon as possible
= in no time	= at once	= instantly

Basic Drills

A 주어진 문장에 어울리는 대답을 고르세요.

1 I'm staying in room 824, but there are a couple of problems.

2 There's something wrong with the Wi-Fi.

3 Is this the Housekeeping Department?

ⓐ I'll send a maintenance man to your room right away.

ⓑ Can you explain what's the matter?

ⓒ Yes, it is. Is there something I can assist you with?

B 괄호 안의 말을 순서대로 배열하여 주어진 의미를 영어로 표현하세요.

1 무엇이 문제인지 설명해 주시겠습니까? (what's / can / explain / the matter / you)

→ ____

2 와이파이에 문제가 있는 것 같아요. (the Wi-Fi / something / with / there's / wrong)

→ ____

3 수리공을 즉시 객실로 보내 드리겠습니다. (to your room / send / right away / a maintenance man / I'll)

→ ____

Buildup Activities 대화를 듣고 빈칸을 채운 후 주어진 질문에 답하세요.

Guest	Hi. Am I speaking with someone in ________________________?
Housekeeping Order Taker	Yes, you are. Do you need some assistance?
Guest	Yes, I do. I'm in room 774. The room has a ________________________ problems.
Housekeeping Order Taker	Can you tell me about them, please?
Guest	Sure. First, the ________________ seems to be broken. I turned on the shower, but I can't get any hot water to come out.
Housekeeping Order Taker	Okay. ________________ is wrong?
Guest	The Wi-Fi ________________ doesn't seem to be working. I can't log on to the Internet.
Housekeeping Order Taker	I'm terribly sorry. A ________________ man will arrive at your room within ten minutes. He'll fix everything.

🎧 09-05

1 **What is the problem with the hot water heater?**

ⓐ It will not turn on.

ⓑ It is making the water too hot.

ⓒ It is not heating any water.

2 **What is the problem with the Wi-Fi?**

ⓐ The password will not work.　　**ⓑ** It keeps logging the guest out.　　**ⓒ** It is working too slowly.

Job Simulation **I**

A 〈보기〉에서 적절한 말을 찾아 각 그림의 상황에 맞는 대화를 완성하세요.

I'm very sorry about that.

This is Housekeeping. What can I do for you?

I'll bring one to your room in just a moment.

1

2

3

B 주어진 세 가지 상황을 이용하여 파트너와 함께 각 상황에 맞는 대화를 연습해 보세요.

Situation	ⓐ	ⓑ	ⓒ
1	some drinking glasses	a notepad	one for you when I arrive
2	a few coffee cups	any coat hangers	five of them for you
3	some bathrobes	any hand towels	you several of them

Guest	Hello. I'm calling from room 201. Is it possible to get ⓐ ______________________ here?
Housekeeping Order Taker	I'll bring them up to you in a few minutes. Do you require anything else?
Guest	There's one more thing. I can't find ⓑ ______________________.
Housekeeping Order Taker	I apologize for the mistake. I shall bring ⓒ ______________________.

Job Simulation Ⅱ

A 〈보기〉에서 적절한 말을 찾아 각 그림의 상황에 맞는 대화를 완성하세요.

1

2

3

B 주어진 세 가지 상황을 이용하여 파트너와 함께 각 상황에 맞는 대화를 연습해 보세요.

Situation	ⓐ	ⓑ
1	be more specific	have someone visit your room
2	tell me about them	send a repair crew there
3	let me know what's wrong	send somebody to room 824

Guest	I'm staying in room 824, but there are a couple of problems.
Housekeeping Order Taker	Can you ⓐ ____________________?
Guest	Sure. First, the shower isn't working properly. There's also something wrong with the Wi-Fi.
Housekeeping Order Taker	I'm very sorry about that. I'll ⓑ ____________________ right away, ma'am.

Reading & Listening

다음 지문을 읽고 음성을 들어 보세요.

🎧 09-06

Housekeeping Department Staff Members and Their Duties

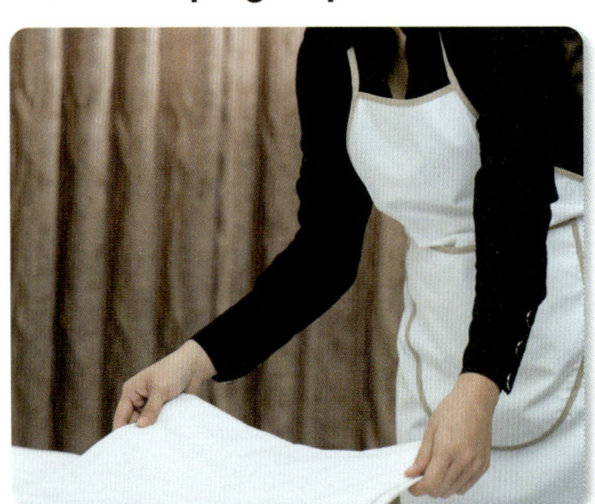

[1]Keeping guests' rooms clean is the job of the Housekeeping Department. These staff members have many duties. The room maids are responsible for making sure that guests' rooms are clean. They change the sheets on the beds, sweep the floors, clean the bathrooms, and pick up trash. Inspectors check the work the room maids do to make sure that there are no problems. Some hotels offer babysitting services, so Housekeeping Department staff members do this job. In addition, a houseman [2]helps room maids carry heavy linens, cleans common areas such as the lobby and hallways, and replenishes supplies in rooms. The Housekeeping Department is responsible for doing guests' laundry, too. So they wash and dry clothes. They also dry-clean and press suits, dresses, and other clothes. Then, other members of the department deliver the clothes to the guests' rooms.

Words & Phrases

sweep to use a broom to clean the floor   **inspector** a person who checks for mistakes or problems   **linens** bedsheets
replenish to provide more supplies   **press** to iron clothes

Basic Grammar

1 5형식 동사 keep

동사 keep은 5형식 동사로서 목적어와 목적격 보어를 취하여 '목적어를 ~한 상태로 유지하다'라는 의미를 나타낸다. 본문에서는 목적격 보어 자리에 형용사가 왔지만 부사, 분사 등도 올 수 있다.

Some rooms are under construction. We will try to keep the noise down.   일부 객실이 공사 중입니다. 소음을 낮게 유지하도록 노력하겠습니다.
They keep the gardens trimmed.   그들은 정원을 손질된 상태로 유지한다.

2 help + 목적어 + (to) V   목적어가 ~하는 것을 돕다

help를 이용하여 '목적어가 ~하는 것을 돕다'라는 의미를 나타낼 수 있다. 이러한 경우, 목적격 보어 자리에는 to부정사가 올 수도 있고 동사원형이 올 수도 있다.

Could you help me (to) buy a ticket for the opera?   제가 오페라 티켓을 구입하는 것을 도와 주시겠어요?
Would you help me (to) fill in this registration card, please?   제가 이 등록 카드를 작성하는 것을 도와 주시겠어요?
The bellman helped me (to) put my luggage in the car.   벨맨이 내가 차에 짐 싣는 것을 도와 주었다.

TIPS & TIPS

환경 보호, 함께 실천해요!

객실의 욕실에는 다양한 종류의 수건이 있습니다. 손용, 얼굴용, 샤워용은 물론이거니와 바닥에 까는 용도로 준비된 수건까지 있습니다. 손님이 원한다면 매일 새로운 수건 세트를 받을 수도 있지요. 하지만 생각해 보면 많게는 수백 개의 객실을 보유한 호텔에서 매일 세탁으로 쓰는 물과 에너지는 어마어마할 것입니다. 그래서 최근에는 많은 호텔이 환경을 생각하여 손님에게 수건 재사용을 권하는 그린카드(Green Card)를 객실에 비치해 두고 있습니다. 이 카드에는 재사용할 수건은 걸어 두고 교체를 원하는 것만 바닥에 둔다면 물을 절약하여 환경을 보호할 수 있다고 쓰여 있습니다. 자신만 쓰는 수건이니 한 번 더 쓴다고 나쁠 것은 없겠지요?

Mistakes and Complaints

UNIT 10

다음은 호텔에 투숙했던 고객의 만족도 평가입니다. 평가를 읽고, 아래 True/False 문제를 풀어 보세요.

Guest Feedback on the Royal Hotel

	Excellent	Good	Average	Poor	Very Poor
Location		✔			
Quality of Welcome	✔				
Cleanliness of Room	✔				
Size of Room					✔
Services	✔				
Facilities		✔			

Comments

Very clean and comfortable with excellent service. But the room was as tiny as a closet. Otherwise, it's a nice hotel in a safe neighborhood and is fairly close to downtown.

1 One of the three most satisfying factors of the hotel is its services. [True / False]

2 What disappointed the guest the most is the size of the room. [True / False]

3 The guest thinks the hotel is far from the center of the city. [True / False]

Vocabulary 주어진 단어와 어울리는 의미를 고르세요.

1 upgrade • • ⓐ to provide something better, often for free

2 specifically • • ⓑ something light eaten before the main course

3 appetizer • • ⓒ a professional cook

4 clearly • • ⓓ on purpose

5 chef • • ⓔ obviously

Warmup Listening 문장을 듣고 그에 맞는 대답을 고르세요.

1 ⓐ No, I stayed in a single. ⓑ No, I want one facing the sea.

2 ⓐ I apologize for the mistake. ⓑ It's a medium-sized hamburger.

3 ⓐ You can use this spoon. ⓑ I'll replace it with another one.

🎧 10-01

Conversation Ⅰ

다음 대화를 듣고 파트너와 함께 대화를 연습해 보세요.

🎧 10-02

Handling Complaints about Wrong Rooms

Front Desk Agent	Hello, Ms. Darden. Is there something I can do for you?
Guest	Yes, there is. I'm afraid you gave me the wrong room.
Front Desk Agent	Could you let me know your room number, ma'am?
Guest	Yes, it's room 312.
Front Desk Agent	Let me check . . . [1] You requested a single room with a lake view, right?
Guest	Yes, room 312 is a single room with a lake view. However, I specifically requested a nonsmoking room, but the room has a strong smell of smoke.
Front Desk Agent	[2] I'm terribly sorry about that, Ms. Darden. Let me find another room for you.
Guest	Okay.
Front Desk Agent	All right . . . [3] I'm going to give you room 509. I've upgraded you to a double room for free.

Key Expressions

1 **You requested a single room with a lake view, right?**   호수 전망의 싱글룸을 요청하셨지요?

손님이 예약한 객실의 유형을 확인하는 문장이다. 객실의 유형은 침대의 크기나 개수, 객실 전망, 흡연 가능 여부에 따라 달라진다.

You are in a twin room with a garden view. Is that correct?   손님께서는 정원 전망의 트윈룸이십니다. 맞으시지요?

2 **I'm terribly sorry about that.**   대단히 죄송합니다.

I'm sorry에 terribly(대단히)라는 부사를 덧붙여 강조의 의미를 더한 표현이다. 뒤에 전치사 about이나 for를 덧붙여 어떤 것에 대해 사과하는지 언급할 수 있다.

I feel really sorry for what happened.   일어난 일에 대해 정말로 죄송합니다.
I apologize for that, sir [ma'am].   그것에 대해 사과 드립니다, 손님.

3 **I'm going to give you room 509.**   509호를 드리겠습니다.

손님에게 객실을 배정할 때 사용할 수 있다. 동사 give 대신에 put이나 move 등도 사용할 수 있다.

I am going to put you in another room.   손님을 다른 객실에 배정해 드리겠습니다.
Would it be okay if I move you to room 212?   제가 손님 객실을 212호로 옮겨 드려도 괜찮으시겠습니까?

💡 Useful Phrases

Could you let me know your room number?   객실 번호를 알려 주시겠습니까?

= What is your room number?   = What room are you in, sir [ma'am]?   = May I ask your room number, please?

Basic Drills

A 주어진 문장에 어울리는 대답을 고르세요.

1 Is there something I can do for you?   •

2 You requested a single room with a lake view, right?   •

3 Could you let me know your room number?   •

• **ⓐ** Yes, room 312 is a single room with a lake view.

• **ⓑ** Yes, it's room 312.

• **ⓒ** I'm afraid you gave me the wrong room.

B 괄호 안의 말을 순서대로 배열하여 주어진 의미를 영어로 표현하세요.

1 호수 전망의 싱글룸을 요청하셨지요? (a single room / right / you / requested / with a lake view)

→ ....

2 대단히 죄송합니다. (terribly / about / sorry / that / I'm)

→ ....

3 509호를 드리겠습니다. (going to / I'm / give / room 509 / you)

→ ....

Buildup Activities 대화를 듣고 빈칸을 채운 후 주어진 질문에 답하세요.

Front Desk Agent	Hello, Mr. Jefferson. Can I assist you with something?
Guest	Yes, you can. I don't believe I got the room __________.
Front Desk Agent	Really? Could you let me know your __________, please?
Guest	Sure. I'm in room 1193.
Front Desk Agent	Just one moment . . . You asked for a double room with a __________ view, right?
Guest	Yes, room 1193 has a great view of the downtown area. However, I reserved a double room, but you gave me a __________ instead.
Front Desk Agent	I apologize for that mistake, sir. Let me get you __________ room immediately.
Guest	Okay.
Front Desk Agent	All right . . . You're now in room 1404. You've been __________ to a suite compliments of the Royal Hotel.

🎧 10-03

1 **What kind of view did the guest request?**

   ⓐ an ocean view   **ⓑ** a river view   **ⓒ** a city view

2 **What does the front desk agent do for the guest?**

   ⓐ upgrade him to a suite   **ⓑ** give him a free night   **ⓒ** give him a free meal

Conversation Ⅱ

다음 대화를 듣고 파트너와 함께 대화를 연습해 보세요.

🎧 10-04

Taking Care of Complaints at a Restaurant

Guest	Excuse me, but there's something wrong with my steak.
Waitress	[1]What seems to be the problem? Doesn't it taste good?
Guest	I don't know. I haven't tried it yet. I ordered my steak cooked medium, but this steak is clearly rare.
Waitress	I apologize for the mistake, sir. [2]Let me take it back to the kitchen and have the chef cook it properly. I'll bring you a free appetizer so that you can have something to eat while you wait.
Guest	Thank you.
Waitress	Is there anything else I can do for you?
Guest	Yes, there is. Could you please bring me another knife? This one doesn't look very clean.
Waitress	Of course. [3]I'll replace it with a new one right away.

Key Expressions

1 What seems to be the problem?   무엇이 문제인 것 같습니까?

문제가 있다고 불만을 표하는 손님에게 정확히 무엇이 문제인지 묻는 표현이다.

What's the matter?   무엇이 문제입니까?
Could you please tell me more specifically about the problem?   문제에 관해 더 구체적으로 말씀해 주시겠습니까?

2 Let me take it back to the kitchen and have the chef cook it properly.

제가 주방으로 다시 가져가서 주방장에게 제대로 요리해 달라고 하겠습니다.

음식에 대해 불만을 표하는 손님에게 음식을 다시 만들어서 내오겠다고 하는 표현이다.

I will take your dish back and bring you a new one.   요리를 다시 가져가고 새 요리를 가져다 드리겠습니다.
Could I take your food and bring you a new bowl of soup?   손님 음식을 가져가고 새 수프를 가져다 드려도 되겠습니까?

3 I'll replace it with a new one right away.   즉시 새것으로 바꿔 드리겠습니다.

새것으로 바꿔 주겠다고 할 때 사용하는 표현으로, '바꾸다'라는 뜻의 동사 exchange를 사용할 수도 있다.

I will replace it with another one.   다른 것으로 바꿔 드리겠습니다.
How about if I exchange it for a new one?   제가 새것으로 바꿔 드리면 어떨까요?

💡 Useful Phrases

스테이크는 얼마나 익혀 드릴까요?

How would you like your steak?	How would you like your steak cooked?
How would you like your steak done?	How would you like your steak broiled?

Basic Drills

A 주어진 문장에 어울리는 대답을 고르세요.

1 Could you please bring me another knife?

2 Excuse me, but there's something wrong with my steak.

3 I ordered my steak cooked medium, but this steak is clearly rare.

ⓐ What seems to be the problem?

ⓑ I apologize for the mistake.

ⓒ I'll replace it with a new one right away.

B 괄호 안의 말을 순서대로 배열하여 주어진 의미를 영어로 표현하세요.

1 무엇이 문제인 것 같습니까? (what / the problem / be / seems to)

→

2 제가 주방으로 다시 가져가서 주방장에게 제대로 요리해 달라고 하겠습니다.
(and / let me / have the chef / take it back / cook it properly / to the kitchen)

→

3 즉시 새것으로 바꿔 드리겠습니다. (replace it / I'll / with / right away / a new one)

→

Buildup Activities 대화를 듣고 빈칸을 채운 후 주어진 질문에 답하세요.

Guest	Pardon me, but there's a problem with my __________.
Waiter	What's the matter with it? Don't you like the food?
Guest	I don't know. I haven't eaten anything yet. I ordered my steak __________, but this steak is well done.
Waiter	I apologize for that oversight. I'll __________ to the kitchen and have the chef cook you another steak. I'll bring you a plate of chicken wings so that you can have some food __________ you wait.
Guest	Thank you.
Waiter	Can I do anything else for you?
Guest	Yes, please. I'd like to have a new __________. This one has a few spots on it.
Waiter	Sure. I'll bring you a __________ in just a second.

🎧 10-05

1 What does the guest complain about?

ⓐ the price of the meal

ⓑ the way the food is cooked

ⓒ the dirtiness of the restaurant

2 What will the waiter bring the guest?

ⓐ a new spoon　　　　ⓑ another plate　　　　ⓒ some dessert

A 〈보기〉에서 적절한 말을 찾아 각 그림의 상황에 맞는 대화를 완성하세요.

보기

I'm going to give you a double room with no bad smells in it.

You reserved a double room with a river view, right?

The room also smells strongly of smoke.

1

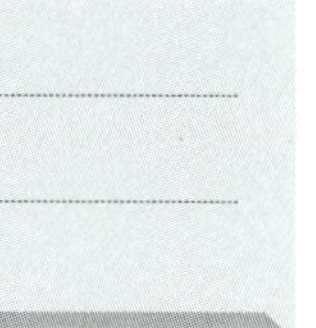

Yes, my room has a river view, but it's a single.

2

I'm very sorry about that.

3

Thank you for solving the problem.

B 주어진 세 가지 상황을 이용하여 파트너와 함께 각 상황에 맞는 대화를 연습해 보세요.

Situation	ⓐ	ⓑ
1	smells strongly of smoke	suite
2	smells like someone was just smoking in it	junior suite
3	smells horrible	triple room

Guest	I specifically requested a nonsmoking room, but the room ⓐ _______________.
Front Desk Agent	I'm terribly sorry about that, Ms. Darden. Let me find another room for you.
Guest	Okay.
Front Desk Agent	All right . . . I'm going to give you room 509. I've upgraded you to a ⓑ _______________ for free.

Job Simulation II

A 〈보기〉에서 적절한 말을 찾아 각 그림의 상황에 맞는 대화를 완성하세요.

보기

I ordered my steak medium, but this is cooked too much.	Yes, I'll bring you a new one at once.	I'll take it back to the kitchen and have the chef cook another one.

1

What's the problem with it?

2

Thank you very much.

3

Could you please replace this fork with another one?

B 주어진 세 가지 상황을 이용하여 파트너와 함께 각 상황에 맞는 대화를 연습해 보세요.

Situation	ⓐ	ⓑ
1	barely cooked	some potato skins
2	very pink in the middle	a bowl of soup
3	medium	some nachos

Guest I ordered my steak well done, but this steak is ⓐ ________________.

Waitress I apologize for the mistake, sir. Let me take it back to the kitchen and have the chef cook it properly. I'll bring you ⓑ ________________ so that you can have something to eat while you wait.

Guest Thank you.

Reading & Listening

다음 지문을 읽고 음성을 들어 보세요.

Steps to Handling Complaints

[1]No matter how hard the hotel staff tries, there will be problems, so some customers will make complaints. Here are the steps hotel staff members should follow when guests are making complaints. First, listen carefully to the customer and say nothing until the customer finishes complaining. Second, ask questions [2]in a concerned manner to learn more details about the problem. Then, put yourself in the customer's shoes and think about how he or she feels at this moment. After that, apologize for the problem, but do not blame anyone in particular. Next, ask the customer how he or she would like you to solve the problem. Feel free to suggest one or two solutions to the problem. Finally, solve the problem or get someone who is capable of solving the problem as quickly as possible.

Words & Phrases

complaint a negative comment; a criticism　**concerned** caring　**put yourself in one's shoes** to imagine that you are another person
blame to accuse someone of doing something bad or wrong　**capable** able to do something

Basic Grammar

1　no matter how + 부사 [형용사]　아무리 ~해도

'no matter how + 부사 [형용사]'는 '아무리 ~해도'라는 뜻으로, 'however + 부사 [형용사]'로도 바꾸어 쓸 수 있다.

No matter how hard the hotel staff tries, there will be problems.　호텔 직원이 아무리 노력해도 문제는 생길 것이다.
→ However hard the hotel staff tries, there will be problems.

2　in a(n) + 형용사 + manner　~한 태도로

'태도', '방식'이라는 뜻의 명사 manner를 사용하여 '~한 태도로'라는 의미를 나타낼 수 있다. manner 대신 way를 사용할 수도 있다.

The manager checked the man on the floor in a worried manner.　지배인은 바닥에 쓰러져 있는 남자를 걱정스러운 태도로 살폈다.
She greets guests in a cheerful way.　그녀는 밝은 태도로 손님들을 맞이한다.

TIPS & TIPS

불만을 칭찬으로 바꾸는 서비스

서비스업체인 호텔은 고객들로터 많은 불만을 듣게 됩니다. 고객의 불만 사항을 처리하는 것은 매우 중요한데, 그 이유는 마이너스 1점을, 0점이 아닌 플러스 1점으로 만들 수 있는 좋은 기회가 되기 때문이지요. 최근에는 많은 사람이 인터넷을 통해 공개적으로 불만을 토로하는데, 그러한 평가는 다른 사람들이 호텔을 선택할 때 악영향을 미치기도 합니다. 그래서 고객이 겪은 문제를 충분히 이해하고, 그에 대한 적절한 사과와 해결책을 제시하는 것이 중요합니다. 인터넷에 떠도는 불만 글을 줄일 수 있을 뿐만 아니라, 불만을 칭찬으로 바꿀 수 있는 소중한 기회가 되기도 하니까요.

Helping Guests

Warmup

다음을 호텔의 분실물 유형에 관한 설명입니다. 각 설명에 해당하는 분실물 유형을 사진에서 고르세요.

1 These will spoil or go bad, so they need to be thrown away soon. ______

2 Guests leave these in their rooms because they do not need to be carried around. ______

3 Guests put these items in safes or safety deposit boxes since they are worth a lot. ______

4 People cannot visit other countries or make purchases without these. ______

ⓐ travel documents

ⓑ perishable items

ⓒ valuable items

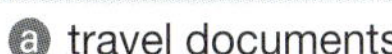

ⓓ non-valuable items

Vocabulary

주어진 단어와 어울리는 의미를 고르세요.

1 alarmed •   • ⓐ injured

2 turn in •   • ⓑ connected to

3 describe •   • ⓒ worried

4 hurt •   • ⓓ to say what someone or something looks like

5 attached to •   • ⓔ to give a lost item to another person

Warmup Listening

문장을 듣고 그에 맞는 대답을 고르세요.

1 ⓐ I have a lot of money in it.   ⓑ It's a black leather wallet.

2 ⓐ I'm sure that he's fine.   ⓑ Can you show me where he is?

3 ⓐ Don't be alarmed.   ⓑ He's of no concern to me.

🎧 11-01

다음 대화를 듣고 파트너와 함께 대화를 연습해 보세요.

🎧 11-02

Lost and Found Service

Guest Excuse me, but I appear to have lost my briefcase. [1] I wonder if you have a lost and found center here.

Concierge We do. [2] Anything people find in the hotel is brought here to the concierge's desk. [3] Can you describe your briefcase, please?

Guest It's a black leather bag, and all of my work documents are in it. My name is written on a tag attached to it.

Concierge May I have your name, sir?

Guest My name is Enrico Marino. I'm in room 641.

Concierge You're in luck, Mr. Marino. Someone turned your briefcase in a few minutes ago. We called your room several times, but nobody answered. Here it is.

Guest Ah, I was in the café looking for my briefcase. Anyway, thanks for returning it.

Concierge It's my pleasure.

Key Expressions

1 I wonder if you have a lost and found center here. 이곳에 분실물 센터가 있는지 궁금해요.

호텔 내에 분실물 센터가 있는지 묻는 말이다. I wonder if ∼를 사용하여 '∼인지 궁금해요'라는 의미를 표현할 수 있다.

Is there a lost and found center here? 여기 분실물 센터가 있나요?

I was wondering if you could help me find my camera. 제 카메라를 찾는 것을 도와 주실 수 있는지 궁금합니다.

2 Anything people find in the hotel is brought here to the concierge's desk.
사람들이 호텔에서 발견한 물건은 무엇이든지 여기 컨시어지 데스크로 옵니다.

호텔에서 발견된 물건은 컨시어지 데스크에 맡겨진다는 표현으로, 분실물 관련 문의에 대한 응답으로 사용할 수 있다.

All lost and found items are brought to the concierge's desk. 모든 분실물은 컨시어지 데스크로 옵니다.

You may be able to find your bag at the concierge's desk. 컨시어지 데스크에서 손님의 가방을 찾을 수 있을지도 모릅니다.

3 Can you describe your briefcase, please? 서류 가방이 어떻게 생겼는지 말씀해 주시겠습니까?

'(∼이 어떠한지) 말하다, 묘사하다'라는 뜻의 동사 describe를 사용하여 분실물의 생김새를 묻는 표현이다.

Could you describe it in detail? 그것이 어떻게 생겼는지 자세히 말씀해 주시겠습니까?

What does it look like? 그것이 어떻게 생겼습니까?

💡 Useful Phrases

It's my pleasure. 별 말씀을요. (상대방의 감사 표현에 응답할 때)

= You're welcome. 　　　= Don't mention it. 　　　= Not at all. 　　　= I am happy to help.

Basic Drills

A 주어진 문장에 어울리는 대답을 고르세요.

1 Can you describe your briefcase, please?

2 May I have your name?

3 We called your room several times, but nobody answered.

ⓐ I was in the café looking for my briefcase.

ⓑ My name is Enrico Marino.

ⓒ It's a black leather bag, and all of my work documents are in it.

B 괄호 안의 말을 순서대로 배열하여 주어진 의미를 영어로 표현하세요.

1 이곳에 분실물 센터가 있는지 궁금해요. (if you / a lost and found center / have / I wonder / here)

→

2 사람들이 호텔에서 발견한 물건은 무엇이든지 여기 컨시어지 데스크로 옵니다.
(in the hotel / is brought here / anything / people find / to the concierge's desk)

→

3 서류 가방이 어떻게 생겼는지 말씀해 주시겠습니까? (can / describe / your briefcase / you / please)

→

Buildup Activities   대화를 듣고 빈칸을 채운 후 주어진 질문에 답하세요.

Guest	Pardon me, but I can't find ____________ anywhere. Does the hotel have a lost and found center?
Concierge	Yes, we do. Anything people find gets brought here to the ____________. Can you tell me what your purse looks like, please?
Guest	It's a ____________ purse with a shoulder strap. It has my credit cards, ID, and some money in it.
Concierge	Can you tell me your name, ma'am?
Guest	I'm Susan Paulson. I'm ____________ in room 384.
Concierge	It's your lucky day, Ms. Paulson. Someone found your purse in the lobby and brought it here ____________. We called your room twice, but nobody picked up the phone. I've got it right here.
Guest	I was at the ____________ searching for it. Anyway, thanks for returning it.
Concierge	You're welcome.

🎧 11-03

1 What did the guest lose?

ⓐ her laptop   ⓑ her passport   ⓒ her purse

2 Where did someone find the guest's missing item?

ⓐ at the restaurant   ⓑ in the lobby   ⓒ by the front door

Conversation II

🎧 11-04

Emergencies and First Aid

Guest	Excuse me, but I need some assistance right away.
Duty Manager	What's the problem, ma'am?
Guest	It's my husband. He was feeling faint, and then he fell down and hit his head on the ground. I think he may be hurt.
Duty Manager	Okay. [1]Could you please take me to him? I need to look at him right away.
Guest	Follow me. He's right over there.
Duty Manager	Hmm . . . Your husband is bleeding heavily. [2]I need to call an ambulance . . . Hello. Please send an ambulance to the Royal Hotel at once. A guest hurt his head and is bleeding badly.
Guest	Is it that serious? I'm really worried.
Duty Manager	[3]Please don't be alarmed. The ambulance will be here soon. In the meantime, let me take care of your husband.

Key Expressions

1 Could you please take me to him? 저를 그분에게 데려가 주시겠습니까?

응급 상황이 발생한 곳으로 안내해 달라는 표현이다.

Would you bring me to him? 저를 그분에게 데려가 주시겠습니까?
Could you tell [show] me where he is? 그분이 어디에 계신지 알려 주시겠습니까?

2 I need to call an ambulance. 구급차를 불러야 합니다.

환자의 상태가 심각해 구급차를 불러야 한다는 표현이다. take to the hospital이나, call 911 등도 응급 상황에서 사용 가능하다.

We need to take [rush] him to the hospital. 이분을 병원으로 데려가야 합니다.
Someone, please call 911! 아무나 911에 전화 좀 해 주세요!

3 Please don't be alarmed. 불안해하지 마세요.

환자의 보호자를 진정시키기 위해 할 수 있는 말이다. 형용사 alarmed 대신 frightened, afraid, scared 등도 사용할 수 있다.

Don't be frightened. 겁먹지 마세요.
Stay calm. 진정하세요.

💡 Useful Phrases

신체적 부상을 나타내는 표현

He fell down and hit his head on the ground. 넘어져서 머리를 바닥에 부딪혔어요.
He slipped and hurt his back. 미끄러져서 허리를 다쳤어요.
He suddenly fainted [passed out / collapsed / lost consciousness]. 갑자기 기절했어요.
He cut his finger. 손가락을 베었어요.
He bruised his shoulder. 어깨에 타박상을 입었어요.

Basic Drills

A 주어진 문장에 어울리는 대답을 고르세요.

1 Is it that serious? I'm really worried. •　　　• ⓐ What's the problem?

2 Could you please take me to him? •　　　• ⓑ Please don't be alarmed.

3 I need some assistance right away. •　　　• ⓒ Follow me. He's right over there.

B 괄호 안의 말을 순서대로 배열하여 주어진 의미를 영어로 표현하세요.

1 저를 그분에게 데려가 주시겠습니까? (me / could you / take / to him / please)

　➡ ____

2 구급차를 불러야 합니다. (to / I / call / an ambulance / need)

　➡ ____

3 불안해하지 마세요. (please / alarmed / be / don't)

　➡ ____

Buildup Activities　대화를 듣고 빈칸을 채운 후 주어진 질문에 답하세요.

Guest	Excuse me. I need some help immediately.
Duty Manager	What's ________________, sir?
Guest	It's my son. He ________________ on the carpet and hit his head against the wall. I think he injured himself.
Duty Manager	Okay. Could you please ________________ where he is? I need to see him.
Guest	Come with me. He's right there.
Duty Manager	Hmm . . . Your son is ________________ a lot. I'm going to call an ambulance . . . Hello. Please send an ambulance to the Royal Hotel immediately. A boy hurt his head and is bleeding badly.
Guest	Is it serious? I'm ________________ about him.
Duty Manager	Please don't ________________. The ambulance will be here momentarily. In the meantime, I'll look after your son.

🎧 11-05

1 What happened to the man's son?

　ⓐ He cut his arm.

　ⓑ He hit a wall.

　ⓒ He broke his leg.

2 Why does the duty manager call an ambulance?

　ⓐ The boy is bleeding a lot.

　ⓑ The guest asked her to do that.

　ⓒ The hotel rules say she must do that.

Job Simulation Ⅰ

A 〈보기〉에서 적절한 말을 찾아 각 그림의 상황에 맞는 대화를 완성하세요.

보 기

| I wonder if there is a lost and found center here. | It's a black leather bag, and all of my work documents are in it. | What do you do with any lost items you find? |

1

Yes, this hotel has one.

2

Anything found in this hotel is taken to the concierge's desk.

3

Could you please describe your briefcase for me?

B 주어진 세 가지 상황을 이용하여 파트너와 함께 각 상황에 맞는 대화를 연습해 보세요.

Situation	ⓐ	ⓑ
1	tell me what your briefcase looks like	You can also see my name written on a tag inside the bag
2	describe your briefcase for me	One of my business cards is taped to the bag
3	tell me what kind of briefcase you have	There's a combination lock on the bag as well

Guest	Excuse me, but I lost my briefcase. I wonder if you have a lost and found center here.
Concierge	We do. Anything people find in the hotel is brought here to the concierge's desk. Can you ⓐ _______________________, please?
Guest	It's a black leather bag, and all of my work documents are in it. ⓑ _______________________.

Job Simulation II

A 〈보기〉에서 적절한 말을 찾아 각 그림의 상황에 맞는 대화를 완성하세요.

What do you recommend doing?

My wife fell on the ground and hurt herself.

Please don't be too worried.

1

Can you please show me where she is?

2

I have to call an ambulance.

3

Is she that seriously injured?

B 주어진 세 가지 상황을 이용하여 파트너와 함께 각 상황에 맞는 대화를 연습해 보세요.

Situation	ⓐ	ⓑ
1	is unconscious	examine him
2	knocked himself out	see how he is doing
3	may need a doctor	look at him

Guest	Excuse me, but I need some assistance right away.
Duty Manager	What's the problem, ma'am?
Guest	It's my husband. He was feeling faint, and then he fell down and hit his head on the ground. I think he ⓐ _______________.
Duty Manager	Okay. Could you please take me to him? I need to ⓑ _______________.

🎧 11 - 06

Medical Emergency Procedures

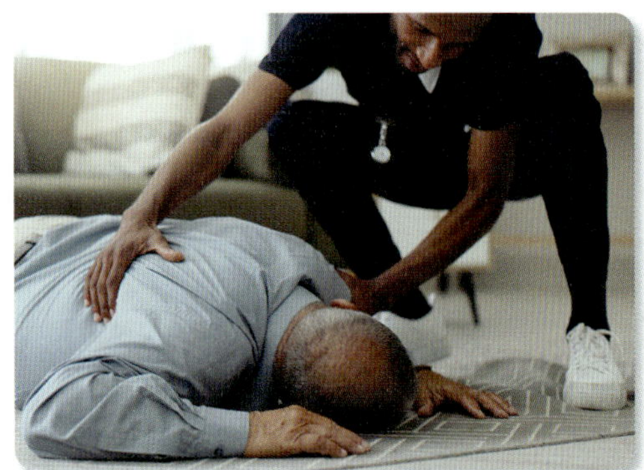

Occasionally, hotel guests suffer medical problems. They are usually minor issues, but guests may also have bigger problems, [1]such as broken bones or heart attacks. All hotel staff members are trained on how to react when there is a medical emergency. First, the staff member [2]should contact the front desk. He or she should describe the emergency and then state the room number or location. The staff member should remain with the guest until help arrives. The front office employee should then contact security. Both a front office employee and someone from the Security Department should hurry to the scene of the incident. Those employees will then determine what to do. They may need to call an ambulance and have the guest taken to the hospital. Or the guest may only need minor assistance that the staff members can take care of at the hotel.

Words & Phrases

issue a problem   **react** to behave in response to something   **state** to say out loud   **remain with** to stay by   **scene** a place; a location

Basic Grammar

1 such as   ~와 같은

such as는 like나 for example처럼 '~와 같은', '예를 들어'라는 뜻을 나타내는 관용구로, 앞서 언급한 명사의 예를 들어 보충 설명을 할 때 사용한다.

The vending machines in the hotel have snacks such as chips, chocolate bars, and cookies.
호텔 자판기에는 감자칩, 초콜릿 바 그리고 쿠키와 같은 스낵이 있다.

Could you tell me more about your hat, such as the color, size, and shape?
손님의 모자에 대해 더 말씀해 주시겠습니까? 예를 들어, 색, 크기 그리고 모양 같은 것 말입니다.

2 '의무'를 나타내는 조동사 should

조동사 should는 '~해야 한다'라는 뜻으로, 도덕적인 의무나 당연히 해야 할 일을 나타낼 때 사용한다. ought to도 같은 의미로 사용할 수 있다.

You should let us know as soon as possible.   가능한 한 빨리 저희에게 알려 주셔야 합니다.
You ought to check with the concierge about the attractions around town.   이 지역 명소에 대해서는 컨시어지와 이야기하셔야 합니다.

TIPS & TIPS

호텔의 안전은 누가 지켜 주나요?

호텔 역시 침입, 절도, 또는 더 심각한 범죄로부터 100퍼센트 안전할 수는 없습니다. 그래서 많은 호텔에는 보안팀이 따로 있습니다. 보안팀은 호텔을 돌며 수상한 사람을 살피기도 하고, 로비나 복도 같은 공공 장소에 설치된 CCTV를 운영하기도 합니다. 최근에는 많은 호텔이 보안을 위해 열쇠 대신 카드키를 사용하고 있습니다. 이 카드키에는 객실 출입 정보가 기록됩니다. 그래서 특정 시각에 누군가 객실에 있었는지 효과적으로 파악할 수 있지요. 또한 호텔은 직원을 채용할 때 각별히 신경을 쓰는 편입니다. 잠재적인 도둑이나 범죄자를 고용하면 큰일이니까요.

Checkout Service

Warmup

다음은 한 고객이 호텔 체크아웃 시 받은 계산서입니다. 계산서를 보고 아래 True/False 문제를 풀어 보세요.

Friday, April 15

Title	Quantity	Per Item	Line Total
Accommodations Charge, 1 Pers., Room 230, 4.11-4.15	4	$130.00	**$520.00**
Dry-Cleaning	1	$20.00	**$20.00**
Massage	2	$50.00	**$100.00**
Buffet Breakfast	3	$20.00	**$60.00**

Total (incl. VAT): $700.00
VAT rate: 19.00%

1 Four people stayed in the hotel room.   [True / False]

2 The guest used the massage service two times.   [True / False]

3 The guest spent twelve dollars on breakfast.   [True / False]

Vocabulary

주어진 단어와 어울리는 의미를 고르세요.

1 charge   •   • ⓐ a fee; money that must be paid for a good or service

2 entire   •   • ⓑ to write one's signature

3 sign   •   • ⓒ complete; total

4 remove   •   • ⓓ to get ready

5 prepare   •   • ⓔ to take off; to get rid of

Warmup Listening

문장을 듣고 그에 맞는 대답을 고르세요.

1 ⓐ Yes, I stayed here.   ⓑ Yes, I had a good time.

2 ⓐ Let me check on that.   ⓑ Here's a snack for you.

3 ⓐ I'll remove that from your bill.   ⓑ I hope you enjoyed your meal.

🎧 12-01

다음 대화를 듣고 파트너와 함께 대화를 연습해 보세요.

🎧 12-02

Checkout Service

Guest	Good morning. I'm here to check out of my room. Here's my room key.
Front Desk Agent	Good morning, Ms. Campbell. [1]Did you enjoy your stay at our hotel?
Guest	Yes, I did. I always enjoy staying at the Royal Hotel.
Front Desk Agent	That's wonderful to hear. [2]Did you use the minibar or have breakfast this morning?
Guest	No, I didn't.
Front Desk Agent	Great. [3]Let me prepare your bill then . . . Here you are.
Guest	Everything looks fine to me. Here's my credit card.
Front Desk Agent	Thank you . . . Would you sign here, please, Ms. Campbell?
Guest	All right.
Front Desk Agent	Here are your card slip and your hotel receipt.
Guest	Thanks. Could you have someone put my bags in the taxi waiting for me outside, please?
Front Desk Agent	Of course. Let me call a bellman over here right now.

Key Expressions

1 Did you enjoy your stay at our hotel? 저희 호텔에서 즐겁게 지내셨습니까?

체크아웃을 하는 손님에게 호텔에서 지내는 동안 즐거운 시간을 보냈는지 묻는 표현이다.

Did you have a good time here, sir [ma'am]? 이곳에서 좋은 시간을 보내셨습니까, 손님?
How was your stay at our hotel? 저희 호텔에서의 숙박은 어떠셨습니까?

2 Did you use the minibar or have breakfast this morning? 오늘 아침에 미니바를 이용하거나 조식을 드셨습니까?

손님이 체크아웃 당일 아침에 미니바를 사용하거나 조식을 먹는 등의 추가 비용이 드는 서비스를 이용했는지 묻는 말이다.

3 Let me prepare your bill then. 그러면 계산서를 준비해 드리겠습니다.

체크아웃을 하는 손님을 위해 계산서를 준비하겠다는 표현으로, '계산서'는 영국식 영어로 bill, 미국식 영어로 check라고 한다.
그 외에 invoice, account, tab 역시 계산서를 의미한다.

Here is your bill, sir [ma'am]. 여기 계산서입니다, 손님.
I will get the check for you. 계산서를 가져다 드리겠습니다.

💡 Useful Phrases

서명을 요청하는 표현

Would you sign here, please? 여기에 서명해 주시겠습니까?
Can [Could] I get your signature here, please? 여기에 손님의 서명을 받을 수 있을까요?
Sign here, please. 여기에 서명해 주십시오.

Basic Drills

A 주어진 문장에 어울리는 대답을 고르세요.

1 Did you use the minibar or have breakfast this morning?

2 Could you have someone put my bags in the taxi waiting for me outside?

3 I always enjoy staying at the Royal Hotel.

- ⓐ No, I didn't.
- ⓑ That's good to hear.
- ⓒ Let me call a bellman over here right now.

B 괄호 안의 말을 순서대로 배열하여 주어진 의미를 영어로 표현하세요.

1 저희 호텔에서 즐겁게 지내셨습니까? (you / did / enjoy / at our hotel / your stay)

→ ____

2 오늘 아침에 미니바를 이용하거나 조식을 드셨습니까? (did you use / the minibar / or / this morning / have breakfast)

→ ____

3 그러면 계산서를 준비해 드리겠습니다. (your bill / let me / then / prepare)

→ ____

Buildup Activities   대화를 듣고 빈칸을 채운 후 주어진 질문에 답하세요.

Guest	Hello. I need to check out. Here's my ____________.
Front Desk Agent	Good morning, Mr. Lee. Did you enjoy your time here?
Guest	Yes, I did. I ____________ here at the Royal Hotel.
Front Desk Agent	I'm glad to hear that. Did you take anything from the ____________ or have breakfast at the restaurant this morning?
Guest	No, I didn't do either.
Front Desk Agent	Great. Let me get your bill ready then . . . Here you are.
Guest	Everything looks fine. Please charge it to my ____________.
Front Desk Agent	No problem . . . Would you sign here, please, Mr. Lee?
Guest	Of course.
Front Desk Agent	Here's your ____________.
Guest	Thank you. What time does the shuttle bus leave for the airport?
Front Desk Agent	I believe the shuttle ____________ in five minutes.

🎧 12_03

1 How does the guest pay for his room?
- ⓐ by charging it to his company
- ⓑ by paying cash
- ⓒ by using his credit card

2 How will the guest go to the airport?
- ⓐ by taxi
- ⓑ by shuttle bus
- ⓒ by subway

🎧 12-04

Handling Disputed Charges

Guest	Pardon me, but I believe there are a couple of mistakes on my bill.
Front Desk Agent	What seems to be the problem?
Guest	I was charged $75 for room service, but I didn't order anything to my room during my entire stay.
Front Desk Agent	[1]Let me check on that, Mr. Chin . . . I'm very sorry, but we made a mistake. [2]Is there anything else wrong on your bill?
Guest	Yes, there's one more thing. I paid this $28 bill at the restaurant last night.
Front Desk Agent	I apologize for that. [3]Let me remove those charges from your bill and give you a new one.
Guest	Thank you very much.
Front Desk Agent	Here you are, Mr. Chin. I apologize again for those terrible mistakes.

Key Expressions

1   Let me check on that.   제가 그것을 확인해 보겠습니다.

어떤 것에 이상이 없는지 확인해 보겠다는 말로, '확인하다'라는 뜻의 check 대신 confirm이나 look into를 쓸 수도 있다.

I'll check what happened.   무슨 일이 있었는지 확인해 보겠습니다.
I'll look into this at once.   이것에 대해 즉시 확인해 보겠습니다.

2   Is there anything else wrong on your bill?   계산서에 또 다른 문제가 있습니까?

손님에게 계산서에 다른 문제는 없는지 묻는 말이다. '실수'라는 뜻의 명사 mistake, error, oversight 등을 사용하여 물어볼 수도 있다.

Did we make any other mistakes?   저희가 또 실수한 것이 있습니까?
Is everything else okay?   다른 것들은 모두 괜찮습니까?

3   Let me remove those charges from your bill and give you a new one.

해당 금액을 손님의 계산서에서 삭제하고 새 계산서를 드리겠습니다.

잘못 계산된 항목을 삭제하고 새로운 계산서를 준비해 주겠다는 표현이다.

I will take those off and make a new bill for you.   그것들을 빼고 새 계산서를 만들어 드리겠습니다.
Allow me to write you a new bill.   제가 새 계산서를 작성해 드리겠습니다

💡 Useful Phrases

I apologize for that.   사과 드립니다.

= I am sorry about that.   = I owe you an apology.   = My apologies.

Basic Drills

A 주어진 문장에 어울리는 대답을 고르세요.

1 I believe there are a couple of mistakes on my bill.

2 I paid this $28 bill at the restaurant last night.

3 Is there anything else wrong on your bill?

ⓐ What seems to be the problem?

ⓑ I apologize for that.

ⓒ Yes, there's one more thing.

B 괄호 안의 말을 순서대로 배열하여 주어진 의미를 영어로 표현하세요.

1 제가 그것을 확인해 보겠습니다. (that / check / on / let / me)

2 계산서에 또 다른 문제가 있습니까? (your bill / wrong / is there / on / anything else)

3 해당 금액을 손님의 계산서에서 삭제하고 새 계산서를 드리겠습니다.
(those charges / a new one / and / let me / from your bill / remove / give you)

Buildup Activities 대화를 듣고 빈칸을 채운 후 주어진 질문에 답하세요.

Guest	I'm sorry, but I think a couple of ________ on this bill are wrong.
Front Desk Agent	What do you believe we made a mistake on?
Guest	I was charged $25 for making an international ________, but I didn't use the phone once while I was here.
Front Desk Agent	Let me check on that, Ms. Davis . . . I'm very sorry, but we made ________. Is there anything else wrong with your bill?
Guest	Yes, one more thing. I paid this $80 bill at the ________ yesterday afternoon.
Front Desk Agent	I'm so sorry. Let me take those ________ off your bill and give you a new one.
Guest	Thank you.
Front Desk Agent	Here you are, Ms. Davis. And I ________ again for the inconvenience.

🎧 12-05

1 What did the guest NOT use during her stay?

ⓐ the television　　　ⓑ the air conditioner　　　ⓒ the telephone

2 What charge did the guest already pay?

ⓐ the minibar fee　　　ⓑ a business center bill　　　ⓒ a phone charge

Job Simulation I

A 〈보기〉에서 적절한 말을 찾아 각 그림의 상황에 맞는 대화를 완성하세요.

보기

| Did you use the minibar or have breakfast today? | Let me get your bill ready. | Yes, I had a wonderful time. |

1

Did you like staying here?

____

2

____

No, I didn't do either of those two things.

3

____

Please take your time.

B 주어진 세 가지 상황을 이용하여 파트너와 함께 각 상황에 맞는 대화를 연습해 보세요.

Situation	ⓐ	ⓑ
1	your receipt	take my luggage outside
2	an itemized bill	carry my bags out to my vehicle
3	a record of your stay here	take my suitcases to the taxi stand

Front Desk Agent	Here's ⓐ _________________________.
Guest	Thanks. Could you have someone ⓑ _________________________, please?
Front Desk Agent	Of course. Let me call a bellman over here right now.

A 〈보기〉에서 적절한 말을 찾아 각 그림의 상황에 맞는 대화를 완성하세요.

보 기

| I'll take those charges off your bill and print a new one. | Are there any other problems with your bill? | Let me check on that, please. |

1

I'm sorry, but I didn't use the minibar at all.

2

Yes, I never ordered room service.

3

Thank you for doing that.

B 주어진 세 가지 상황을 이용하여 파트너와 함께 각 상황에 맞는 대화를 연습해 보세요.

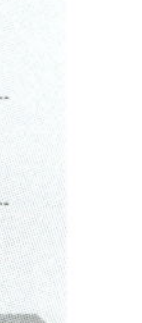

Situation	ⓐ	ⓑ	ⓒ
1	order anything to my room	Do you see any other problems	for dry-cleaning
2	touch the minibar	Is there anything else you disagree with	for a massage
3	eat or drink any of the items in the minibar	Did we make any other errors	at the bar

Guest   I was charged $75 for room service, but I didn't ⓐ __________ during my entire stay.

Front Desk Agent   Let me check on that, Mr. Chin . . . I'm very sorry, but we made a mistake. ⓑ __________ ?

Guest   Yes, there's one more thing. I paid this $28 bill ⓒ __________ last night.

Front Desk Agent   I apologize for that. Let me remove those charges from your bill and give you a new one.

Servicing a Room for the Next Guest

After a guest checks out, the room maid has to [1]get the room ready for the next guest. The room maid has a checklist to follow to be sure that everything is properly prepared. First, the room maid needs to air out the room and put cleaner in the toilet. Next, the room maid confirms that the guest [2]left nothing behind, takes the sheets off the bed, and checks them for any problems. After that, the room maid picks up trash in the room, makes the bed, and cleans the bathroom. Then, the room maid puts clean towels and a new roll of toilet paper in the bathroom and also puts mini bars of soap and small bottles of shampoo in the bathroom. The room maid replaces the food and the drinks in the minibar and refrigerator, checks the room for damage, and resets the air conditioner. Then, the room maid vacuums the entire room and sprays some air freshener in it. Lastly, the room maid turns in any valuable items that the previous guest left behind.

Words & Phrases

checklist a list of activities to do　**confirm** to check on something　**mini** very small　**damage** destruction; injury
valuable worth a lot of money

Basic Grammar

1 get + 목적어 + 형용사 [p.p.]　목적어를 ~한 상태로 만들다

동사 get은 'get + 목적어 + 형용사 [p.p.]' 형태의 5형식 동사로 쓰여 '목적어를 ~한 상태로 만들다'라는 뜻을 나타낼 수 있다.

Please get the bill prepared for Mr. Robinson.　로빈슨 씨를 위해 계산서를 준비해 주세요.
I can ask a staff member to get it done for you.　제가 직원 한 명에게 그것을 하도록 요청할 수 있습니다.

2 leave ~ behind　~을 두고 가다 [오다]

동사 leave(~을 남기다)가 '뒤에'라는 뜻의 부사 behind와 함께 쓰여, '뒤에 남기다', 즉 '무엇인가를 어떠한 장소에 남기고 가다[오다]'라는 뜻을 이루는 구동사이다.

Guests often leave their valuable belongings behind.　손님들은 자주 귀중품을 두고 간다.
I am calling about a smartphone that I might have left behind.　제가 놓고 온 것 같은 스마트폰 때문에 전화했는데요.

TIPS & TIPS

빨리 빨리 체크아웃하게 해 주세요!

아침에 늦게 일어나 한시라도 빨리 공항에 가야 하는 손님이 있습니다. 그런데 프런트 데스크는 체크아웃하려는 손님들로 가득하니, 이걸 어쩌면 좋지요? 걱정하지 마세요. 이런 손님을 위해 신속하게 체크아웃을 할 수 있는 호텔의 서비스가 있습니다. 바로 익스프레스 체크아웃(Express Checkout) 서비스인데요, 이 서비스를 원하는 손님은 보통 체크아웃 전날 밤에 호텔로부터 계산서를 받습니다. 계산서에 문제가 없다면 다음 날 프런트 데스크에 와서 체크아웃하면 됩니다. 또는 체크아웃 당일 아침에 프런트 데스크에 방문하여 그 자리에서 영수증만 받고 즉시 체크아웃을 할 수도 있습니다. 이 경우에는 줄을 설 필요가 없습니다. 어떻게 보면 일반적인 방법과 많이 다른 것 같진 않지만, 일분일초가 아까운 손님에는 탁월한 서비스가 아닐까요?

Answer Key

UNIT 01 Answering Questions about Hotels

p.9

Warmup

1 wheelchair ramp
2 free parking
3 Wi-Fi access
4 hotel shuttle bus

Vocabulary

1 ⓓ   2 ⓐ   3 ⓔ
4 ⓒ   5 ⓑ

Warmup Listening

`Script` 🎧 01-01

1 How may I help you?
2 What about parking?
3 What's the best way to get there?

1 ⓐ
2 ⓐ
3 ⓑ

Conversation Ⅰ

p.10

Basic Drills

A

1 ⓒ
2 ⓐ
3 ⓑ

B

1 How may I help you?
2 Which facilities would you like to know about?
3 There are wheelchair ramps at every entrance.

Buildup Activities

`Script` 🎧 01-03

Front Desk Agent Thank you for calling the Royal Hotel. What can I help you with today?

Guest Good afternoon. I'm thinking about staying at your hotel. But I need to know about the facilities there first.

Front Desk Agent Of course. I understand. What would you like to ask about?

Guest Does your hotel have assistance for the blind?

Front Desk Agent Yes, we do. There are signs posted in Braille everywhere. And some rooms are especially equipped for the blind.

Guest That sounds excellent. How about the elevators?

Front Desk Agent All of the buttons in our elevators have Braille written on them. We are very popular with visually impaired guests. We take good care of them.

Guest Thank you for the information. I'll contact you later to make a reservation.

1 ⓐ
2 ⓑ

Conversation Ⅱ

p.12

Basic Drills

A

1 ⓒ
2 ⓑ
3 ⓐ

B

1 The easiest way is to take our shuttle bus.
2 In that case, you can take either a city bus or a rideshare.
3 It takes around thirty minutes to get here by car.

Buildup Activities

`Script` 🎧 01-05

Front Desk Agent Royal Hotel. You are speaking with Chris. How may I assist you?

Guest Hello. I'm going to go from the airport to your hotel. What's the fastest way there?

Front Desk Agent The fastest way is to take our shuttle bus. You can catch it in front of Exit 5. It operates from 6:00 AM until 8:00 PM.

Guest My plane is arriving late at night, so I can't use the shuttle bus.

Front Desk Agent Hmm . . . You'd better take a bus or a rideshare then.

Guest Can you give me some <u>details</u> about each one?

Front Desk Agent Sure. It will <u>cost</u> about $30 to come here in a rideshare. It will take about 25 minutes if you ride in a car. If you take the bus, get on the number 10 bus. It will be a one-hour ride.

Guest The rideshare sounds <u>better than</u> the bus. Thanks for telling me about everything.

1 ⓑ
2 ⓑ

Job Simulation Ⅰ — p.14

A

1 I'm thinking of reserving a room at your hotel.
2 Which facilities are you interested in?
3 That sounds wonderful.

Job Simulation Ⅱ — p.15

A

1 The best way is to ride on the shuttle bus.
2 Can you let me know about them, please?
3 A car ride here will take about half an hour.

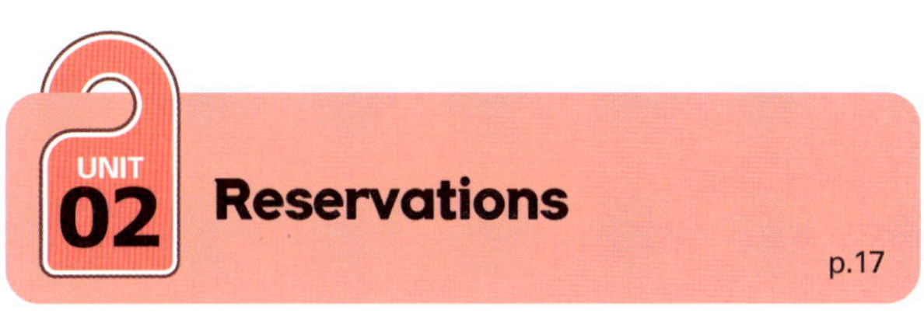

UNIT 02 Reservations — p.17

Warmup

1 ⓑ
2 ⓐ
3 ⓒ

Vocabulary

1 ⓑ	2 ⓔ	3 ⓒ
4 ⓐ	5 ⓓ	

Warmup Listening

Script 🎧 02-01

1 Are there any rooms available?
2 May I have your name, please?
3 How do you want to change your reservation?

1 ⓑ
2 ⓑ
3 ⓐ

Conversation Ⅰ — p.18

Basic Drills

A

1 ⓑ
2 ⓐ
3 ⓒ

B

1 You can get a double room for the discounted rate of $89 if you stay here two or more nights.
2 May I please have your name?
3 Could you spell that, please?

Buildup Activities

Script 🎧 02-03

Guest Good morning. I tried to book a room online but couldn't. I want to get a room for this weekend. Are there any <u>available</u>?

Reservation Clerk Let me see . . . Yes, we still have a few rooms available. And we're offering a special <u>promotion</u> this weekend.

Guest Is that so? What is it?

Reservation Clerk If you stay here for two or more nights, you can get a double room for only $89. That's <u>half off</u> the normal rate. It also comes with a free daily breakfast and free parking.

Guest What a great <u>deal</u>. I'd like a double room for this Saturday and Sunday <u>night</u>, please.

Reservation Clerk Great. Could you please tell me your name, sir?

Guest My name is Jason Hampton.

Reservation Clerk I'm sorry, but how do you <u>spell</u> your last name?

Guest It's H-A-M-P-T-O-N.

1 ⓒ

2 ⓑ

Conversation **II**   p.20

Basic Drills

1 ⓒ

2 ⓐ

3 ⓑ

B

1 Could you please repeat your name?

2 I think we have a bad connection.

3 How would you like to change your reservation?

Buildup Activities

Script 🎧 02 - 05

> **Reservation Clerk** Royal Hotel. Tom speaking. May I help you?
>
> **Guest** Hello. I need to change my reservation. I'm Susan Daley, and I have a reservation for this Thursday.
>
> **Reservation Clerk** I'm sorry, but could you please tell me your name again? There was some static on the line.
>
> **Guest** Of course. My name is Susan Daley. My reservation number is PTR59-087.
>
> **Reservation Clerk** Thank you very much, Ms. Daley. What change would you like to make?
>
> **Guest** I'm supposed to check in on Thursday, but I can't go there until this Friday. I will stay at your hotel from Friday until next Monday morning.
>
> **Reservation Clerk** I changed your reservation, Ms. Daley. Do you need anything else this morning?
>
> **Guest** No, thank you. I appreciate your assistance.

1 ⓐ

2 ⓑ

Job Simulation **I**   p.22

A

1 We're offering double rooms for only $100 if you stay for at least two nights.

2 Could you let me know your name, please?

3 Of course. It's G-E-O-R-G-E S-C-H-M-I-D-T.

Job Simulation **II**   p.23

A

1 Could you say your name one more time?

2 Let me repeat my name then.

3 I want to extend my stay by four days.

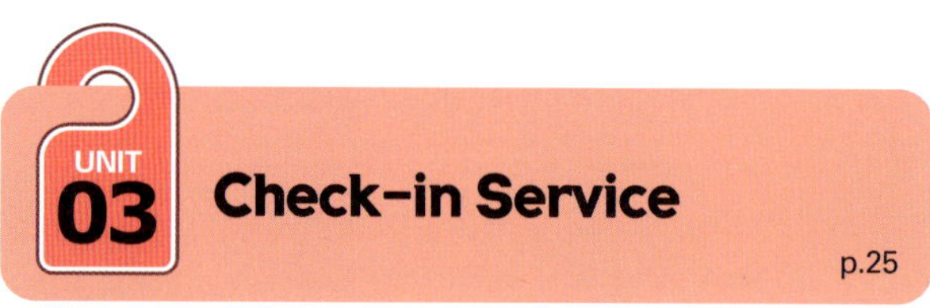

UNIT **03** Check-in Service
p.25

Warmup

1 luggage cart

2 registration form

3 key card

4 call bell

Vocabulary

1 ⓓ   **2** ⓐ   **3** ⓔ

4 ⓑ   **5** ⓒ

Warmup Listening

Script 🎧 03 - 01

> **1** You reserved a suite for two days, right?
>
> **2** Would you rather have a smoking or nonsmoking room?
>
> **3** Do you have some picture ID?

1 ⓐ

2 ⓑ

3 ⓑ

Conversation **I**   p.26

Basic Drills

A

1 ⓑ

2  ⓒ

3 ⓐ

B

1 Do you have a reservation?

2 You'll be staying with us in a deluxe room for three nights, right?

3 Would you prefer a smoking or nonsmoking room?

Buildup Activities

 **Script** 🎧 03-03

Guest Good evening. I would like a room, please.

Front Desk Agent Hello, sir. Do you have a reservation here?

Guest Yes, I do. I booked a room online last night. Here is my information.

Front Desk Agent Thank you. Let me check everything . . . Welcome to the Royal Hotel, Mr. Yamagata. You reserved a single room for four nights. Is that correct?

Guest Yes, it is.

Front Desk Agent May I please see your passport and a credit card?

Guest I have them right here.

Front Desk Agent Thank you. Would you like a smoking or nonsmoking room?

Guest A nonsmoking room would be perfect.

1 ⓒ

2 ⓐ

p.28

Basic Drills

A

1  ⓑ

2 ⓐ

3 ⓒ

B

1 I'm sorry to hear that.

2 May I see some type of picture ID, please?

3 Could you please fill out this registration form?

Buildup Activities

Script 🎧 03-05

Guest Hello. Can I please get a room?

Front Desk Agent Did you make a reservation?

Guest No, I didn't. I am checking in because my connecting flight got canceled. I was scheduled to leave today, but I won't be able to depart until tomorrow evening.

Front Desk Agent I'm terribly sorry about that, ma'am. Maybe you can visit a couple of museums before you leave. It's your lucky day. We have one room left. Is a single room okay?

Guest Yes, a single room is perfect.

Front Desk Agent Great. Do you have some form of picture ID? I need you to fill out this registration form as well.

Guest Of course. Here is my passport. May I borrow a pen, please?

Front Desk Agent Yes, here you are.

1 ⓑ

2 ⓒ

p.30

A

1 Did you make a reservation?

2 You reserved a suite for two nights, didn't you?

3 Would you like to have a smoking room or a nonsmoking room?

p.31

A

1 I'm very sorry about your flight, sir.

2 Do you have some type of picture ID?

3 Can you fill out this registration form, please?

UNIT 04 Giving Essential Information about Hotel Services

p.33

Warmup

1 ⓓ
2 ⓒ
3 ⓐ
4 ⓑ

Vocabulary

1 ⓔ   2 ⓑ   3 ⓓ
4 ⓐ   5 ⓒ

Warmup Listening

Script 🎧 04-01

> 1 When is breakfast served here?
> 2 How can I get laundry service?
> 3 What other services does the hotel have?

1 ⓑ
2 ⓐ
3 ⓑ

Conversation Ⅰ

p.34

Basic Drills

Ⓐ

1 ⓒ
2 ⓐ
3 ⓑ

Ⓑ

1 Just take a left as soon as you get off the elevator.
2 Our hotel restaurant serves breakfast from 5:00 to 10:30 AM.
3 Your room reservation includes a complimentary breakfast for two each day.

Buildup Activities

Script 🎧 04-03

> **Front Desk Agent** Here's your key card, Ms. Chin. Your room is on the tenth floor. You can take the

elevator right behind you. All you have to do is turn right once you get off the elevator.

Guest Thank you. By the way, what time can I have breakfast?

Front Desk Agent The hotel restaurant provides breakfast from 5:00 to 11:00 AM. You can find it on the fourth floor.

Guest How much is breakfast?

Front Desk Agent Actually, your room reservation comes with a complimentary breakfast every day. So the breakfast buffet costs nothing. Do you want to know anything else?

Guest Yes, I have another question. How can I get room service?

Front Desk Agent Dial 0 from your room telephone. Then, you can order anything from the menu twenty-four hours a day.

1 ⓑ
2 ⓒ

Conversation Ⅱ

p.36

Basic Drills

Ⓐ

1 ⓐ
2 ⓑ
3 ⓒ

Ⓑ

1 We also have a fitness center, a wellness center, and a swimming pool on the third floor.
2 You can order room service 24 hours a day.
3 Dial 0 if you need anything.

Buildup Activities

Script 🎧 04-05

> **Bellman** Follow me, ma'am. Please allow me to escort you to your room.
>
> **Guest** Thank you so much.
>
> **Bellman** I'd like to tell you a bit about the hotel's facilities. The restaurant and two bars are located on the second floor. The fitness center, the wellness center, and the swimming pool are all on the fifth floor.
>
> **Guest** That sounds great. I'd like to go to the

wellness center for a massage later tonight. What other services does the hotel have?

Bellman It's possible to order room service 24 hours a day. We have a business center on the ninth floor, too.

Guest Excellent. I appreciate you telling me everything.

Bellman It's my pleasure. Here we are. This is your room, ma'am. After you, ma'am . . . Shall I put your bags over here?

Guest Yes, that would be perfect.

Bellman Your room telephone is here. Dial 5 if you require anything.

1 ⓑ
2 ⓐ

Ⓐ

1 Take a right when you get out of the elevator.

2 You can get breakfast anytime between 5:00 and 10:00 AM.

3 How much does breakfast cost?

Ⓐ

1 The hotel has a fitness center, a spa, and a swimming pool.

2 You can order room service anytime and also have your laundry done.

3 All you have to do is dial 0.

UNIT 05 Giving Local Information
p.41

Warmup

1 taxi
2 bus
3 subway

Vocabulary

1 ⓑ   2 ⓔ   3 ⓐ
4 ⓓ   5 ⓒ

Warmup Listening

Script ∩ 05 - 01

1 What's the best way there?
2 Where can I get a tram card?
3 Where do you suggest that I go?

1 ⓐ
2 ⓑ
3 ⓐ

Basic Drills

Ⓐ

1 ⓐ
2 ⓒ
3 ⓑ

Ⓑ

1 There is a taxi stand located right in front of the hotel.

2 It usually costs around 25 euros to get to the heart of downtown.

3 You need to purchase a tram card for each member of your family.

Buildup Activities

Script ∩ 05 - 03

Guest Good morning. Can you help me, please?

Concierge With pleasure. What can I assist you with?

Guest I'd like to take my family to the theater district to go sightseeing. How should we go there?

Concierge The fastest way is by taking a rideshare. You can have a car pick you up in front of the hotel. It should cost about 30 euros to get to that part of town.

Guest What about the bus? Is there a bus stop nearby?

Concierge Yes, there is. There's a bus stop one block from here. I've got a schedule for the bus here. But you need to purchase a transportation card for everyone in your family.

Guest Where can I buy them?

Concierge The hotel's gift shop sells them. Please follow me. I'll take you there.

1 ⓑ
2 ⓒ

Conversation Ⅱ p.44

Basic Drills

A

1 ⓒ
2 ⓐ
3 ⓑ

B

1 I highly recommend the museum of natural history.
2 Why don't you go to the museum of natural history?
3 Let me write the address and directions for you.

Buildup Activities

Script 🎧 05-05

Guest I'd like to go sightseeing downtown today. Where do you think I should go?

Concierge What about art galleries? The city has several good ones. I strongly suggest that you visit the national art gallery.

Guest That sounds good. What else should I check out?

Concierge As you may know, this is a very old city with many historical sites. A tour of some ancient ruins and castles is leaving from here in ten minutes. It lasts all day.

Guest I don't have time for that. I need to meet a client at three.

Concierge I see. Then why don't you go to the national art gallery? After that, you can go to your business meeting from there.

Guest Okay. Thanks for the suggestion. How can I get there?

Concierge I'll show you where it is on this map.

1 ⓐ
2 ⓑ

Job Simulation Ⅰ p.46

A

1 There are always taxis at the hotel's front door.
2 How much is it to go downtown by taxi?
3 You need to buy a tram card for everyone taking it.

Job Simulation Ⅱ p.47

A

1 I strongly believe you should visit the city's museum.
2 Why don't you go to the local art gallery?
3 Can you tell me how to get there?

UNIT 06 Restaurant & Bar Service
p.49

Warmup

1 ⓐ, ⓒ
2 ⓑ, ⓕ
3 ⓓ, ⓔ

Vocabulary

1 ⓓ   2 ⓔ   3 ⓑ
4 ⓐ   5 ⓒ

Warmup Listening

Script 🎧 06-01

1 Are you a guest here?
2 How about if I order from the menu?
3 What would you like to drink?

1 ⓑ
2 ⓐ
3 ⓑ

Basic Drills

A

1 ⓑ

2 ⓐ

3 ⓒ

B

1 Would you like to have the breakfast buffet or see a menu?

2 Are you a guest at the hotel?

3 What if I want to order from the menu instead?

Buildup Activities

Script 🎧 06-03

Waitress Good morning. Welcome to the Skyview restaurant. Would you prefer to have the breakfast buffet or to see a menu?

Guest Good morning. Actually, I haven't made up my mind yet.

Waitress Are you staying here at the hotel?

Guest Yes, I am. Why?

Waitress All hotel guests receive a complimentary breakfast buffet. The buffet has many kinds of foods. For example, you can get cereal, waffles, bacon, sausages, eggs, yogurt, and fruit.

Guest Wow, that's a good deal. But what if I decide to order from the menu instead?

Waitress In that case, you will have to pay money. So do you want to order from the a la carte menu?

Guest That's all right. I think I'll just have the buffet.

1 ⓒ

2 ⓑ

Conversation II   p.52

Basic Drills

A

1 ⓒ

2 ⓑ

3 ⓐ

B

1 What can I get you to drink?

2 We have Vanguard, Daeng, and a couple of local beers on tap.

3 A mimosa is half orange juice and half champagne.

Buildup Activities

Script 🎧 06-05

Bartender Good evening, ma'am. Would you care for something to drink?

Guest Hi there. What draft beers do you have?

Bartender We have Vanguard, Daeng, and three local beers on tap.

Guest Hmm . . . Maybe I'll order something else.

Bartender How about having a margarita or a mint julep? Both are popular drinks with many customers.

Guest What's in a mint julep? I've never had one before.

Bartender A mint julep contains whiskey, sugar cubes, and mint leaves. Making it is simple, and it tastes great.

Guest Okay. I'll try one of those, please.

1 ⓐ

2 ⓒ

Job Simulation I   p.54

A

1 I haven't made up my mind yet.

2 Yes. What makes you ask that?

3 You need to pay for your breakfast if you do that.

Job Simulation II   p.55

A

1 What would you like to have?

2 We have several local beers on tap.

3 It's a combination of vodka and orange juice.

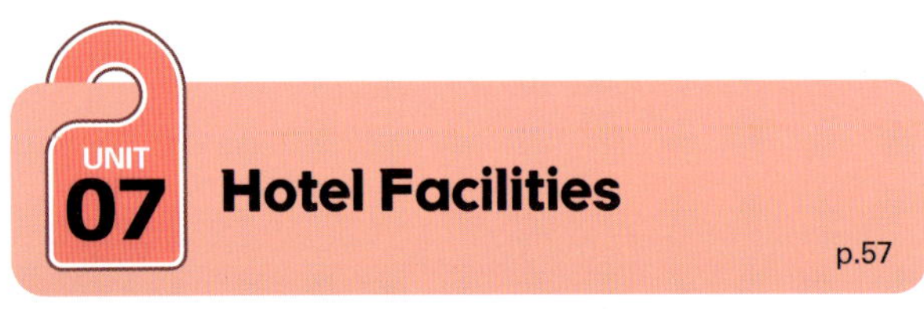

UNIT 07 Hotel Facilities

p.57

Warmup

1 ⓒ
2 ⓓ
3 ⓐ
4 ⓑ

Vocabulary

1 ⓔ   2 ⓓ   3 ⓒ
4 ⓐ   5 ⓑ

Warmup Listening

Script 🎧 07-01

1 What room are you staying in?
2 Where can I change into my gym clothes?
3 Can you arrange a translator for me?

1 ⓑ
2 ⓐ
3 ⓑ

Conversation I

p.58

Basic Drills

A

1 ⓐ
2 ⓑ
3 ⓒ

B

1 What is your room number?
2 The men's dressing room is over there to the right.
3 To get to it, go through that door on the left.

Buildup Activities

Script 🎧 07-03

Fitness Center Attendant Welcome to the fitness center at the Royal Hotel. Could you tell me your room number, please?

Guest Sure. I'm in room 303. I'm Kelly Hopkins.

Fitness Center Attendant Thank you, Ms. Hopkins. Do you need me to tell you how to use any of the equipment here?

Guest No, I don't. I work out at a gym regularly. But can you tell me where the changing room is?

Fitness Center Attendant Of course. The dressing room is on the other side of the room.

Guest Thank you. Can I shower there as well?

Fitness Center Attendant Yes, you can. We also have a sauna. It's located behind the cycling machines.

Guest Thanks a lot for your assistance.

1 ⓒ
2 ⓑ

Conversation II

p.60

Basic Drills

A

1 ⓐ
2 ⓑ
3 ⓒ

B

1 You spoke with me.
2 Do you know how to use it?
3 Can you arrange one for me?

Buildup Activities

Script 🎧 07-05

Guest Good afternoon. I'm Jessica Stewart. I called this morning about using the scanner.

Business Center Attendant Yes, Ms. Stewart. You talked to me. The scanner is over there. Do you require any assistance with it?

Guest That's all right. I know how to use it.

Business Center Attendant Excellent. Can I do anything else for you?

Guest Yes, please. Would you make 20 copies of this report for me? I need 3 color copies.

Business Center Attendant Of course. I'll start doing that right now.

Guest I need something else, too. I require a Russian translator for a meeting tomorrow at one. Can you find one for me?

Business Center Attendant That will be no problem at all. Let me make the copies first. Then, I will make the necessary arrangements for a translator.

1 ⓐ
2 ⓒ

Job Simulation I
p.62

1 What room are you staying in?
2 Where can I put on my gym clothes?
3 How can I get to the sauna?

Job Simulation II
p.63

1 I called the business center a while ago.
2 Is there anything else I can do for you?
3 Yes, I'll do that in just a couple of minutes.

UNIT 08 Room Service
p.65

1 minibar
2 air conditioner
3 bathrobe
4 in-room safe

Vocabulary

1 ⓑ   2 ⓐ   3 ⓓ
4 ⓒ   5 ⓔ

Warmup Listening

Script  08-01

1 What would you like to have?
2 Are you going to charge this to your room?
3 Should I put them on the floor over here?

1 ⓐ
2 ⓐ
3 ⓑ

Conversation I
p.66

Basic Drills

A

1 ⓑ
2 ⓐ
3 ⓒ

B

1 What would you like to order?
2 Will you be charging this to your room?
3 Someone will deliver the food to your room in about twenty minutes.

Buildup Activities

Script 08-03

Guest Hello. I'm Paul Stewart in room 357. May I please order some room service?

Telephone Operator Yes, you may. What would you like to have, sir?

Guest I'll take the sirloin steak dinner. I'd also like a baked potato with it.

Telephone Operator All right. Would you care for something to drink?

Guest Yes, please. I want some iced tea, please.

Telephone Operator No problem. How will you be paying for your meal?

Guest I'll pay cash. What's the total?

Telephone Operator Your meal costs $35. Your food will be delivered within fifteen minutes.

1 ⓐ
2 ⓑ

Basic Drills

A

1 ⓒ

2 ⓐ

3 ⓑ

B

1 I'm sorry, but there must be some mistake.

2 The Royal Hotel provides guests on their honeymoon with a complimentary bottle of champagne and a box of chocolates.

3 Shall I put them here on the table?

Buildup Activities

Script 🎧 08-05

Room Service Clerk Good evening. Room service.

Guest I'm sorry, but you must be mistaken. I never called room service to order anything.

Room Service Clerk That's right. But you're here on your honeymoon, aren't you?

Guest That's right.

Room Service Clerk The Royal Hotel provides honeymooners with a complimentary bottle of champagne as well as some roses.

Guest Thank you so much. That's a nice gesture.

Room Service Clerk Should I put these on the table here? I've got some ice and two glasses as well.

Guest That's perfect. Thanks a lot. My husband and I really appreciate it.

1 ⓐ

2 ⓑ

A

1 What food would you like to order?

2 No, I'll pay for it with my credit card.

3 Someone will visit your room twenty minutes from now.

A

1 I'm sorry, but I think you made a mistake.

2 The Royal Hotel gives honeymooners complimentary champagne and chocolate.

3 Shall I put your items on this table?

UNIT 09

Housekeeping Service

p.73

Warmup

1 bed making

2 babysitting

3 laundry

Vocabulary

1 ⓓ   **2** ⓒ   **3** ⓐ

4 ⓑ   **5** ⓔ

Warmup Listening

Script 🎧 09-01

1 How may I be of service to you?

2 Can you explain the problem?

3 What else is wrong?

1 ⓐ

2 ⓑ

3 ⓑ

Basic Drills

A

1 ⓒ

2 ⓑ

3 ⓐ

B

1 This is Housekeeping.

2 I'll bring them up to you in a few minutes.

3 I apologize for the mistake.

Buildup Activities

Script 09-03

Housekeeping Order Taker Good afternoon. Housekeeping. What can I do for you?

Guest Hello. I'm calling from room 409. Can someone bring some more pillows to my room?

Housekeeping Order Taker Didn't the maid already leave some on the bed in your room?

Guest Yes, she did, but I need three more, please.

Housekeeping Order Taker I see. Someone will deliver them in a couple of minutes. Can I do anything else for you?

Guest Yes, you can. There's no shampoo in the bathroom.

Housekeeping Order Taker I'm really sorry about that. I'll bring a couple of bottles along with your towels.

Guest Thanks a lot. I appreciate it.

1 ⓑ

2 ⓑ

Conversation II   p.76

Basic Drills

A

1 ⓑ

2 ⓐ

3 ⓒ

B

1 Can you explain what's the matter?

2 There's something wrong with the Wi-Fi.

3 I'll send a maintenance man to your room right away.

Buildup Activities

Script 09-05

Guest Hi. Am I speaking with someone in Housekeeping?

Housekeeping Order Taker Yes, you are. Do you need some assistance?

Guest Yes, I do. I'm in room 774. The room has a couple of problems.

Housekeeping Order Taker Can you tell me about them, please?

Guest Sure. First, the hot water heater seems to be broken. I turned on the shower, but I can't get any hot water to come out.

Housekeeping Order Taker Okay. What else is wrong?

Guest The Wi-Fi password doesn't seem to be working. I can't log on to the Internet.

Housekeeping Order Taker I'm terribly sorry. A maintenance man will arrive at your room within ten minutes. He'll fix everything.

1 ⓒ

2 ⓐ

Job Simulation I   p.78

A

1 This is Housekeeping. What can I do for you?

2 I'll bring one to your room in just a moment.

3 I'm very sorry about that.

Job Simulation II   p.79

A

1 Can you explain what they are?

2 The shower isn't working properly.

3 I'll have a maintenance man visit your room to fix it.

UNIT 10 Mistakes and Complaints   p.81

Warmup

1 True

2 True

3 False

Warmup Listening

`Script` 🎧 10-01

> 1   You asked for a double room facing the mountains, right?
>
> 2   I ordered my hamburger rare, but this is medium.
>
> 3   This fork looks a bit dirty.

1   ⓑ

2   ⓐ

3   ⓑ

Conversation Ⅰ   p.82

Basic Drills

Ⓐ

1   ⓒ

2   ⓐ

3   ⓑ

Ⓑ

1   You requested a single room with a lake view, right?

2   I'm terribly sorry about that.

3   I'm going to give you room 509.

Buildup Activities

`Script` 🎧 10-03

> **Front Desk Agent**   Hello, Mr. Jefferson. Can I assist you with something?
>
> **Guest**   Yes, you can. I don't believe I got the room I requested.
>
> **Front Desk Agent**   Really? Could you let me know your room number, please?
>
> **Guest**   Sure. I'm in room 1193.
>
> **Front Desk Agent**   Just one moment . . . You asked for a double room with a city view, right?
>
> **Guest**   Yes, room 1193 has a great view of the downtown area. However, I reserved a double room, but you gave me a single room instead.
>
> **Front Desk Agent**   I apologize for that mistake, sir. Let me get you another room immediately.
>
> **Guest**   Okay.
>
> **Front Desk Agent**   All right . . . You're now in room 1404. You've been upgraded to a suite compliments of the Royal Hotel.

1   ⓒ

2   ⓐ

Conversation Ⅱ   p.84

Basic Drills

Ⓐ

1   ⓒ

2   ⓐ

3   ⓑ

Ⓑ

1   What seems to be the problem?

2   Let me take it back to the kitchen and have the chef cook it properly.

3   I'll replace it with a new one right away.

Buildup Activities

`Script` 🎧 10-05

> **Guest**   Pardon me, but there's a problem with my meal.
>
> **Waiter**   What's the matter with it? Don't you like the food?
>
> **Guest**   I don't know. I haven't eaten anything yet. I ordered my steak medium rare, but this steak is well done.
>
> **Waiter**   I apologize for that oversight. I'll take it back to the kitchen and have the chef cook you another steak. I'll bring you a plate of chicken wings so that you can have some food while you wait.
>
> **Guest**   Thank you.
>
> **Waiter**   Can I do anything else for you?
>
> **Guest**   Yes, please. I'd like to have a new spoon. This one has a few spots on it.
>
> **Waiter**   Sure. I'll bring you a new one in just a second.

1   ⓑ

2   ⓐ

Job Simulation Ⅰ   p.86

 **A**

1 You reserved a double room with a river view, right?

2 The room also smells strongly of smoke.

3 I'm going to give you a double room with no bad smells in it.

Job Simulation Ⅱ   p.87

A

1 I ordered my steak medium, but this is cooked too much.

2 I'll take it back to the kitchen and have the chef cook another one.

3 Yes, I'll bring you a new one at once.

UNIT 11

Helping Guests

p.89

Warmup

1 ⓑ

2 ⓓ

3 ⓒ

4 ⓐ

Vocabulary

1 ⓒ   2 ⓔ   3 ⓓ

4 ⓐ   5 ⓑ

Warmup Listening

`Script` 🎧 11 - 01

1 Can you describe your wallet, please?

2 My husband fell down and hit his head.

3 I'm really concerned about him.

1 ⓑ

2 ⓑ

3 ⓐ

Conversation Ⅰ   p.90

Basic Drills

A

1 ⓒ

2 ⓑ

3 ⓐ

B

1 I wonder if you have a lost and found center here.

2 Anything people find in the hotel is brought here to the concierge's desk.

3 Can you describe your briefcase, please?

Buildup Activities

`Script` 🎧 11 - 03

Guest Pardon me, but I can't find my purse anywhere. Does the hotel have a lost and found center?

Concierge Yes, we do. Anything people find gets brought here to the concierge's desk. Can you tell me what your purse looks like, please?

Guest It's a brown leather purse with a shoulder strap. It has my credit cards, ID, and some money in it.

Concierge Can you tell me your name, ma'am?

Guest I'm Susan Paulson. I'm staying in room 384.

Concierge It's your lucky day, Ms. Paulson. Someone found your purse in the lobby and brought it here five minutes ago. We called your room twice, but nobody picked up the phone. I've got it right here.

Guest I was at the restaurant searching for it. Anyway, thanks for returning it.

Concierge You're welcome.

1 ⓒ

2 ⓑ

Conversation Ⅱ   p.92

Basic Drills

A

1 ⓑ

2 ⓒ

3 ⓐ

B

1 Could you please take me to him?

2 I need to call an ambulance.

3 Please don't be alarmed.

Buildup Activities

Script 🎧 11-05

Guest Excuse me. I need some help immediately.

Duty Manager What's the matter, sir?

Guest It's my son. He tripped on the carpet and hit his head against the wall. I think he injured himself.

Duty Manager Okay. Could you please show me where he is? I need to see him.

Guest Come with me. He's right there.

Duty Manager Hmm . . . Your son is bleeding a lot. I'm going to call an ambulance . . . Hello. Please send an ambulance to the Royal Hotel immediately. A boy hurt his head and is bleeding badly.

Guest Is it serious? I'm worried about him.

Duty Manager Please don't be alarmed. The ambulance will be here momentarily. In the meantime, I'll look after your son.

1 ⓑ

2 ⓐ

Job Simulation Ⅰ
p.94

A

1 I wonder if there is a lost and found center here.

2 What do you do with any lost items you find?

3 It's a black leather bag, and all of my work documents are in it.

Job Simulation Ⅱ
p.95

A

1 My wife fell on the ground and hurt herself.

2 What do you recommend doing?

3 Please don't be too worried.

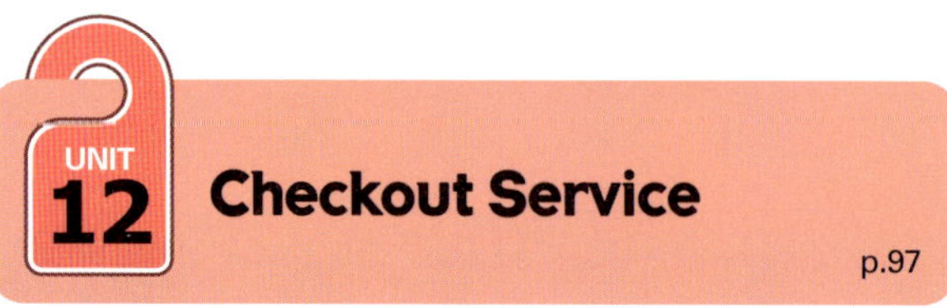

UNIT 12 Checkout Service
p.97

Warmup

1 False

2 True

3 False

Vocabulary

1 ⓐ   2 ⓒ   3 ⓑ

4 ⓔ   5 ⓓ

Warmup Listening

Script 🎧 12-01

1 Did you enjoy staying here?
2 I didn't eat or drink anything from the minibar.
3 I paid this charge at the restaurant yesterday.

1 ⓑ
2 ⓐ
3 ⓐ

Conversation Ⅰ
p.98

Basic Drills

A

1 ⓐ
2 ⓒ
3 ⓑ

B

1 Did you enjoy your stay at our hotel?

2 Did you use the minibar or have breakfast this morning?

3 Let me prepare your bill then.

Buildup Activities

Script 🎧 12-03

Guest Hello. I need to check out. Here's my room key.

Front Desk Agent Good morning, Mr. Lee. Did you enjoy your time here?

Guest Yes, I did. I love staying here at the Royal Hotel.

Front Desk Agent I'm glad to hear that. Did you take anything from the minibar or have breakfast at the restaurant this morning?

Guest No, I didn't do either.

Front Desk Agent Great. Let me get your bill ready then . . . Here you are.

Guest Everything looks fine. Please charge it to my company's account.

Front Desk Agent No problem . . . Would you sign here, please, Mr. Lee?

Guest Of course.

Front Desk Agent Here's your receipt.

Guest Thank you. What time does the shuttle bus leave for the airport?

Front Desk Agent I believe the shuttle leaves in five minutes.

1 ⓐ

2 ⓑ

p.100

Basic Drills

A

1 ⓐ

2 ⓑ

3 ⓒ

B

1 Let me check on that.

2 Is there anything else wrong on your bill?

3 Let me remove those charges from your bill and give you a new one.

Buildup Activities

Script 🎧 12-05

Guest I'm sorry, but I think a couple of items on this bill are wrong.

Front Desk Agent What do you believe we made a mistake on?

Guest I was charged $25 for making an international phone call, but I didn't use the phone once while I was here.

Front Desk Agent Let me check on that, Ms. Davis . . . I'm very sorry, but we made an error. Is there anything else wrong with your bill?

Guest Yes, one more thing. I paid this $80 bill at the business center yesterday afternoon.

Front Desk Agent I'm so sorry. Let me take those charges off your bill and give you a new one.

Guest Thank you.

Front Desk Agent Here you are, Ms. Davis. And I apologize again for the inconvenience.

1 ⓒ

2 ⓑ

p.102

A

1 Yes, I had a wonderful time.

2 Did you use the minibar or have breakfast today?

3 Let me get your bill ready.

p.103

A

1 Let me check on that, please.

2 Are there any other problems with your bill?

3 I'll take those charges off your bill and print a new one.

Appendix: Word List

facility (n) 시설
something that serves a specific purpose

consider (v) 고려하다, 생각하다
to think about

wheelchair access (n) 휠체어 접근 용이성
the state of being able to be visited by a person in a wheelchair

ramp (n) 경사로
a sloping surface that connects two different levels

floor (n) 층
a level in a building; a story

handicapped (adj) 장애가 있는
disabled; having some sort of disability

front door (n) 현관, 정문
the main entrance to a building

call back (phr) 다시 전화하다
to return a person's telephone call

the blind (n) 시각장애인들
people who cannot see

posted (adj) (벽 등에) 붙어 있는
hanging up on a wall or door

Braille (n) 점자
a language for the blind

equipped (adj) 갖춘, 구비된
having something useful

visually impaired (adj) 시각 장애가 있는
unable to see well or at all; blind

take good care of (phr) ~을 잘 돌보다, 충분히 신경 쓰다
to look after well

be of service (phr) 돕다
to help; to assist

run (v) 운행하다
to operate

fare (n) 요금
the money one pays to take a bus or taxi

catch (v) (택시 등을) 잡아타다
to be able to take a bus, taxi, or other form of transportation

ride (v) (차량에) 타다
to take some form of transportation

get on (phr) ~을 타다
to get on board a bus, train, or plane

available (adj) 이용할 수 있는
empty; free

check (v) 확인하다
to see if something is right; to confirm

promotional (adj) 홍보의, 판촉의
relating to publicity

offer (n) 할인
a deal

discounted (adj) 할인된
on sale; cheaper than normal

rate (n) 가격
a price

stay (v) 묵다, 머무르다
to remain in a place

include (v) 포함하다
to contain

complimentary (adj) 무료의
free

daily (adj) 매일의
happening every day

good deal (n) 좋은 거래, 저렴한 가격
a special offer; a good price

offer (v) 제공하다, 제안하다
to propose; to suggest

half (n) 반, 2분의 1
fifty percent of something

normal (adj) 정상의, 통상적인
usual; regular

come with (phr) ~이 딸려 있다
to include; to go together

repeat (v) 한 번 더 말하다
to say or do again

connection (n) (전화의) 연결
a link

require (v) 필요하다
to need

static (n) 잡음
interference on a telephone line

check in (phr) (호텔 등에) 체크인하다
to sign in to a hotel

put into (phr) ~에 입력하다, 집어넣다
to enter onto a computer; to add

deluxe room (n) 디럭스룸
a hotel room that is nicer than normal; a luxury room

correct (adj) 맞는, 정확한
right; accurate

prefer (v) 선호하다, 원하다
to like one thing more than another

nonsmoking room (n) 금연실
a hotel room in which people may not smoke

reserve (v) 예약하다
to save; to guarantee for the future

online (adv) 온라인에서
while connected to the Internet

walk-in (n) 예약하지 않고 방문한 손님
a person with no reservation but who wants to stay at a hotel

connecting flight (n) 연결편
a second airplane flight a person must take

cancel (v) 취소하다
to stop; to give up

sights (n) 관광지, 명소
interesting places to see in an area

depart (v) 떠나다
to leave

be in luck (phr) 운이 좋다
to be lucky; to be fortunate

a couple of (phr) 몇 개의; 두 개의
a few; two

picture ID (n) 사진이 있는 신분증
a piece of identification with a person's picture on it

fill out (phr) (서식 등을) 채우다, 기입하다
to complete something such as a form

registration form (n) 등록 양식
an official sheet of paper a person must complete to do something

driver's license (n) 운전면허증
a type of ID allowing a person to drive a vehicle

terribly (adv) 매우
very

borrow (v) 빌리다
to use for a short period of time and then to return to its owner

UNIT 04

take a left (phr) 좌회전하다
to turn to the left

get off (phr) ~에서 내리다
to get out of

serve (v) 제공하다
to provide food

be located (phr) 있다, 위치하다
to be in a certain place

pay (v) 지불하다
to use money to buy something

laundry (n) 세탁물
clothes

dial (v) 전화하다
to call a telephone number

visit (v) 방문하다
to go to see

pick up (phr) ~을 수거하다
to collect; to get something from another person or place

behind (prep) ~의 뒤에
in back of

provide (v) 제공하다
to offer; to sell

come with (phr) ~이 딸려 있다
to include

cost (v) (비용이) 들다
to require a certain amount of money to buy

room service (n) 룸서비스
the serving of food and drinks in a hotel room

order (v) 주문하다
to buy; to purchase

escort (v) 동행하다, 바래다주다
to go with a person to a place

fitness center (n) 피트니스 센터
a gym; a health club

business center (n) 비즈니스 센터
a place in a hotel where people can do business

allow (v) 허락하다
to let; to permit

bar (n) 바
a place serving drinks

UNIT 05

local (adj) 현지의, 지역의
native

downtown (adv) 시내로, 시내에
to or in the main area of a city

the heart of (phr) ~의 중심
the middle of

tram (n) 트램, 전차
a streetcar

purchase (v) 구매하다
to buy

gift shop (n) 기념품 가게
a store that sells souvenirs

go sightseeing (phr) 관광하다
to tour an area

cab (n) 택시
a taxi

nearby (adv) 근처에
close

advise (v) 조언하다, 권하다
to give guidance to

suggest (v) 제안하다
to propose

museum (n) 박물관
a place in which items of interest are displayed

recommend (v) 추천하다, 권하다
to suggest; to advise

in that case (phr) 그렇다면, 그런 경우에는
therefore

art gallery (n) 미술관
a museum that displays art

next to (phr) ~ 옆에
beside; by

directions (n) 가는 방법
instructions

check out (phr) (흥미로운 것을) 보다, 살펴보다
to have a look at

historical (adj) 역사적인
being important in history

show (v) 보여 주다, 알려 주다
to point out; to indicate

UNIT 06

breakfast (n) 조식, 아침 식사
a meal eaten in the morning

buffet (n) 뷔페
a meal in which people can eat as much of various kinds of foods as they want

decide (v) 결정하다
to choose

extra (adj) 추가의
more than normal; bonus

a la carte (adj) 메뉴에서 고르는, 일품 요리의
with a separate price for each item on a menu

receive (v) 받다
to get

draft beer (n) 생맥주
beer that comes from a barrel or cask

a couple of (phr) 몇 개의; 두 개의
a few; two

local (adj) 현지의, 지역의
native

on tap (phr) (맥주 등이) 통 안에 준비되어 있는
ready to be drawn from a barrel or cask

popular (adj) 인기 있는
well-liked

drink (n) 음료
a liquid that people consume

be familiar with (phr) ~을 알다
to know about; to know well

champagne (n) 샴페인
a type of sparkling white wine

simple (adj) 쉬운, 간단한
easy

taste (v) 맛이 ~하다
to have a certain flavor

care for (phr) ~을 좋아하다, 원하다
to like; to want

contain (v) 들어 있다
to have

whiskey (n) 위스키
an alcoholic liquor made from grain

cube (n) 정육면체 모양인 것
a solid that has six equal sides

UNIT 07

equipment (n) 기구, 장비
machinery; a tool

change into (phr) ~으로 갈아입다
to change clothes; to put on

workout clothes (n) 운동복, 체육복
clothes that a person exercises in

dressing room (n) 탈의실
a changing room

go through (phr) ~을 통과하다
to pass through; to enter

gym (n) 헬스클럽; 체육관
a health club; a place where people exercise or play sports

regularly ad (v) 자주, 정기적으로
often; commonly

cycling machine (n) 사이클 기구
an exercise bike

fax machine (n) 팩스기
a machine that can send images over a telephone line

send (v) 보내다
to transmit; to mail

copy (v) 복사하다
to make a duplicate

black-and-white (adj) 흑백의
having only the colors black and white

staple (v) 스테이플러로 고정하다
to connect papers together by using a piece of metal

get on (phr) ~을 하다
to do

translator (n) 통역사; 번역가
a person who can change speech from one language into another

arrange (v) 준비하다, 마련하다
to set up; to reserve; to prepare

take care of (phr) ~을 처리하다
to do; to look after

report (n) 보고서
a statement; an account

necessary (adj) 필요한
needed

arrangement (n) 준비, 마련
preparation

UNIT 08

room service (n) 룸서비스
the serving of food and drinks in a hotel room

French fries (n) (프랑스식) 감자튀김
sliced potatoes that are fried in oil

charge (v) 청구하다
to defer a payment until a later time

total (n) 총액, 합계
an overall price or number

cost (v) (값이) ~이다
to require a certain amount of money to buy

deliver (v) 배달하다
to take from one place to another to give to a person

sirloin (n) (소의) 등심
a cut of beef

baked (adj) 구운
cooked in an oven

meal (n) 식사
food that a person eats

mistake (n) 착오, 실수
an error

honeymoon (n) 신혼 여행
a trip people go on after they get married

provide (v) 제공하다
to give

bottle (n) 병
a glass container

champagne (n) 샴페인
a type of sparkling white wine

thoughtful (adj) 친절한, 배려심 있는
considerate

bring (v) 가지고 오다
to carry; to take

glass (n) 유리잔
a cup from which a person can drink liquid

mistaken (adj) 잘못 알고 있는, 오해한
in error

honeymooner (n) 신혼 여행자
a person on his or her honeymoon

gesture (n) (의도를 표현하는) 행위
an action to show good intentions

Housekeeping (n) 객실관리부
the cleaning department at a hotel

bring ~ up (phr) ~을 가져다 주다
to deliver

apologize (v) 사과하다
to say that one is sorry

bar (n) (막대 형태의 초콜릿·비누 등을 가리키는) 바
a small piece of something solid

maid (n) 객실 청소 담당자
a cleaning woman

leave (v) 두고 가다
to drop off

explain (v) 설명하다
to describe

wrong (adj) 잘못된
not right; incorrect

work (v) 작동하다
to operate; to run

properly (adv) 제대로
correctly

turn on (phr) ~을 켜다
to send power to a machine

flicker (v) 깜박거리다
to blink

turn off (phr) ~을 끄다
to stop operating

annoying (adj) 짜증스러운, 성가신
bothersome

send (v) 보내다
to order a person to go somewhere

maintenance man (n) 수리공
a person who repairs tools and equipment

broken (adj) 고장 난
not working properly

cool down (phr) ~을 시원하게 하다
to make cold

bother (v) 신경 쓰이게 하다
to annoy; to pester

arrive (v) 도착하다
to get to; to reach

handle (v) 처리하다, 다루다
to take care of

complaint (n) 불만, 불평
a criticism; a negative comment

specifically (adv) 명확하게
exactly; precisely

upgrade (v) 상위 등급으로 높여 주다
to make better

assist (v) 돕다
to help

ask for (phr) ~을 요청하다, 요구하다
to request

immediately (adv) 즉시
now; at once

compliments of (phr) ~이 주는
given by

steak (n) 스테이크
high-quality beef

well done (adj) 완전히 익힌
cooked thoroughly

clearly (adv) 분명히
obviously; apparently

rare (adj) 설익은, 덜 구워진
cooked so that the meat is still red or pink on the inside

take ~ back (phr) ~을 다시 가져가다
to return

chef (n) 주방장, 요리사
a professional cook

appetizer (n) 애피타이저
food one eats before the main course

clean (adj) 깨끗한
spotless; not dirty

replace (v) 교체하다
to exchange one thing for another

oversight (v) 실수
a mistake; an error

stuff (v) (음식에) 소를 채우다
to fill

spot (n) 얼룩; 점
a stain

lose (v) 잃어버리다
to be unable to find

wonder (v) 궁금해하다
to be curious about

describe (v) 묘사하다
to explain what someone or something looks like

attached to (phr) ~에 붙어 있는
connected to

case (n) 케이스
a bag

purse (n) 핸드백
a woman's handbag

pick up the phone (phr) 전화를 받다
to answer a telephone call

search for (phr) ~을 찾다
to look for

first aid (n) 응급 처치
basic treatment given to injured people

fall down (phr) 넘어지다
to drop to the ground or a lower position

hurt (adj) 다친
injured

take a look at (phr) ~을 보다
to see if a person is fine

bleed (v) 피를 흘리다
to have blood coming from one's body

ambulance (n) 구급차
a vehicle that takes people to hospitals

badly (adv) 심하게, 몹시
seriously

alarmed (adj) 불안해하는
worried

trip (v) 발을 헛디디다
to stumble and fall while walking

wall (n) 벽
an upright construction that supports a ceiling

momentarily (adv) 곧, 금방
for a short time

look after (phr) ~을 돌보다
to take care of

UNIT 12

stay (n) 머무름, 방문
a visit

bill (n) 계산서
a statement showing how much money one owes

fine (adj) 괜찮은
okay; all right

sign (v) 서명하다
to write one's signature

slip (n) (작은) 종이 조각
a small piece of paper

receipt (n) 영수증
a sheet of paper indicating what a person bought and how much the person paid

glad (adj) 기쁜, 즐거운
happy; pleased

get ~ ready (phr) ~을 준비하다
to prepare

account (n) 외상 계정
a service given to a customer allowing that person to charge items and to pay for them later

shuttle bus (n) 셔틀 버스
a bus that travels between two places regularly

believe (v) 생각하다
to think

entire (adj) 전체의; 완전한
total; complete

pay (v) 지불하다
to use money to buy a good or service

remove (v) 삭제하다, 없애다
to get rid of; to erase

charge (n) 청구 금액, 요금
a fee; money that must be paid for a good or service

international (adj) 국제의
relating to another country

make a phone call (phr) 전화를 하다
to use the telephone

error (n) 실수, 잘못
a mistake

take ~ off (phr) ~을 빼다
to remove; to get rid of

inconvenience (n) 불편
trouble